The Relentless
Mercy of God

The Relentless Mercy of God

by

Joseph V. Corpora, C.S.C.

The Relentless Mercy of God

Copyright © 2017 by Joseph V. Corpora C.S.C.

10 9 8 7 6 5 4 3 2

ISBN 978-0-9961362-7-3

Published by
CORBY BOOKS
P.O. Box 93
Notre Dame, IN 46556

Manufactured in the United States of America

*Dedicated to
Pope Francis and to my Dear Mom and Dad*

Table of Contents

Foreword

O ne of the earliest accounts of Christian pilgrimage dates back to the fourth century after Christ. A woman named Egeria left her home, probably in Galicia (now northwest Spain) and walked across Europe, stopping in Constantinople before finally entering the gates of the holy city, Jerusalem. It appears that she made that long and difficult journey alone but wanted to share its fruits with her friends back home.

Egeria wrote a long letter to a group of women in Galicia, describing in detail her pilgrimage, lingering lovingly on her experience of the holy places while providing a personal witness to the social reality of her time. The letter is the oldest known report of religious pilgrimage written by a woman.

The Relentless Mercy of God is also the account of a pilgrimage. Although the author, Father Joe

Corpora, C.S.C., provides details of trips to Rome, the Holy Land, Mexico and even Seattle, Washington, the journey that unites his narrative is the great Jubilee of Mercy, which began on December 8, 2015 and concluded on November 20, 2016. You will read his account of this yearlong pilgrimage, the places he visited and the people whose hearts he touched. Like Egeria, Father Joe will describe the food that sustained him, but also his wonder at the way the God he loves so unabashedly manifests himself today.

Pope Francis announced the Jubilee of Mercy with a 28-page letter that begins with a solemn pronouncement as well as a surprising claim: "Jesus is the face of the Father's mercy. These words might well sum up the mystery of the Christian faith." He invited the Church to embark on a Holy Year "dedicated to living out in our daily lives the mercy" which God "constantly extends to all of us."

Father Joe played a unique role in the great Jubilee, since Pope Francis named him as a "Missionary of Mercy." After announcing the Jubilee, the Holy Father selected priests from each region of the world to be special ambassadors that would preach, teach and celebrate the gift of God's mercy. Pope Francis granted these missionaries the authority to pardon even those sins, which normally would require the special absolution that is reserved to the Holy See. They were to be "living signs of the Father's readiness to welcome those in search of his pardon."

In the pages of this charming book, Father Joe tells the story of that pilgrimage of mercy. His mission takes him to people who live on the fringes of the Church, like Guatemalan immigrants in the state of Washington or the LGBT community on the campus of a great Catholic university. He also meets people who apparently live at the center, such as the many priests he was able to help. These women and men became fellow pilgrims, not simply the recipients of Father Joe's ministry and message. They helped him understand the beautiful power of a "culture of encounter" that is a mutual exchange of gifts.

His fellow pilgrims taught Father Joe a curious lesson about the gift of mercy: that you cannot tell yourself about mercy anymore than you can tickle yourself! Some things in life necessarily demand the help of others.

In telling the message of mercy, Father Joe meditates on some of the parables of Jesus with fresh insight. He encourages the reader to allow these stories to speak with new force, rather than presume that you already know what the Teacher intends to say. With Father Joe's help, these stories will resonate within you, provoking surprise, delight and gratitude.

Nearing the conclusion of her own holy travelogue, our friend from the fourth century, Egeria, promised to keep her sisters back home informed about where she would go and what future marvels she might see. We should ask the same kindness of a Missionary of Mercy for our times: that my dear friend, Father Joe Corpora, continue to give witness to the marvels of mercy that he sees the Lord accomplishing each day. Who knows? As he speaks to us about the relentless mercy of God, our hearts may begin to burn.

Cardinal Joseph W. Tobin, C.Ss.R.
ARCHBISHOP OF NEWARK

Introduction

When Pope Francis wrote his Apostolic Letter, *Misericordiae Vultus*, and released it on April 15, 2015 (Divine Mercy Sunday), announcing the Year of Mercy, no one could have predicted the revolution of love and tenderness that it would set off in the Church and in the world. Since the first days of his Pontificate, the Holy Father has repeatedly preached and talked about the mercy of God. He has repeatedly said, "We might get tired of asking God for forgiveness, but God never tires of forgiving us." Pope Francis will be forever remembered as "the Mercy Pope" and his Pontificate as "a time of mercy for all."

For a very long time I have I sought more the mercy of God than the love of God. I do not know why. Perhaps, it might be because mercy seems so unmerited, so unearned, so gratuitous and so necessary for a sinner like me. "I am a sinner whose sins are forgiven" has been my unwavering self-understanding for many years. God just gives us his mercy because he wants to, because he loves us so much. It is all a gift.

During this Year of Mercy many people have asked me, "Well, since you are a Missionary of Mercy, can you give me a definition for mercy?" I usually say something like this: I'm not sure I can define it, but I can recognize it. And I can tell you what mercy is not.

Mercy is not pity. It is not patronizing. It is not feeling sorry for another person. It is not looking down on someone. And it is certainly not caring about someone as though mercy only goes one way, from me to the other person. Mercy is not saying "oh, that poor person."

Mercy is empathy, kindness, compassion, forgiveness, tenderness, and much more. It is generous, lavish and freely given. When the Holy Father talks about mercy he often refers to it as oil being massaged into someone—soaking someone in the oil of mercy.

The world cannot exist without mercy. As R.C. Lewontin wrote,

> According to a Haggadic legend, when God decided to create the world he said to

Justice, "Go and rule the earth which I am about to create." But it did not work. God tried seven times to create a world ruled by Justice, but they were all failures and had to be destroyed. Finally, on the eighth try, God called in Mercy and said, "Go, and together with Justice, rule the world that I am about to create because a world ruled only by Justice cannot exist." This time, apparently, it worked, more or less.[1]

One might say that mercy makes the world go 'round.

Sometimes you hear that too much mercy (as though there can be too much of it!) doesn't allow for justice. This is not true. In his book *The Name of God Is Mercy* Pope Francis says that even justice must be understood in the light of God's mercy.

Mercy is bigger and broader and deeper and stronger than anything else. In the end, we will all be saved by the relentless mercy of God. I don't think that anyone will be able to escape this mercy, for "it is not the will of the Father that any one of these little ones should perish" (Matthew 18:14).

---

[1] *Happy Are They...Living the Beatitudes in America*, Jim Langford, page 9.

I was extremely humbled and excited and encouraged when Pope Francis appointed me to serve as a Missionary of Mercy. I have received a lifetime of mercy, and now I would have the opportunity to extend that mercy, to be a vessel of God's relentless mercy, to perhaps help others believe in and accept God's mercy.

The Holy Spirit has given so much fruit to the Church through the Year of Mercy. The Year of Mercy grew and grew and grew throughout the year—getting bigger and bigger. Towards the end of the Year, people were wondering and asking if the Pope might extend the Year of Mercy into another year.

* * * * *

Why did the Year of Mercy take off, so to speak? We all need mercy. We all stand in desperate need of God's mercy. No one can live without mercy. You cannot have a world without mercy. In the end we will all be saved by the free and relentless mercy of God.

I truly believe God has given me the grace to write about mercy, and I have really enjoyed doing so. As in my other presentations about mercy, I might be the biggest beneficiary, because I realize more and more that I truly believe what I say and write about the mercy of God.

Every priest has inside of him one core homily, and mine is mercy—the free, relentless mercy of God. If you listen closely to my homilies, this theme will come through again and again. What follows in this little book are essays and reflections about God's mercy and what it has been like to serve the Church as a Missionary of Mercy. There is no specific order to them. I only hope that my readers will accept the mercy of God at a deeper level with each essay, and then extend that mercy to those around them.

May Jesus, the face of the Father's mercy, open your life to his relentless mercy as we pray:

Lord Jesus Christ, Son of the Living God,
have mercy on me, a sinner.

Acknowledgements

A t the invitation of John Nagy of *Notre Dame
Magazine*, I began to write about mercy. He
asked if I might write a reflection about mercy every
three to four weeks for the web version of *Notre Dame
Magazine*. I am very grateful to John for encouraging me to write these essays. I'm also very grateful to
Jim Langford and Tim Carroll for offering to publish
them into this little volume. And I especially would
like to thank my friend Cardinal Joseph Tobin for
kindly agreeing to write the Foreword to this book.

There are many other people to thank and acknowledge—my parents, Dominick and Evelyn Mo-
sellie Corpora, my brother Jim, and my sister Mary
Grace. Most of all I wish to thank God who makes
everything possible. Since we all live in God and have

our being in God, by thanking God no one is left out.

*To God, be all glory, honor, praise and thanksgiving,
now and for ages unending.*

Being Mercy:
Reflections on My Trip to Rome to Be Commissioned as a Misssionary of Mercy in this Jubilee Year of Mercy

I arrived in Rome on Sunday morning, February 7, 2016. The flight had been safe and easy, but long, from Atlanta to Rome. By 10:00 a.m. I was at the Hotel Columbus, which is less than 100 yards from the Vatican—a totally great location. After washing up I went to St. Peter's for the Sunday noon Angelus. Like clockwork the famous window opened and Pope Francis appeared in the window while thousands and thousands of people in St. Peter's Square cheered and clapped, waved flags and banners. The Holy Father greeted everyone, gave a brief homily on the Sunday Gospel, then prayed the Angelus, gave the Apostolic blessing and then recognized a few groups here and there. What is it about seeing the Pope that would draw thousands and thousands of people to come to St. Peter's for 12 minutes? There is no doubt that this Pope draws more people than others. I love him.

After the Angelus, I went to a nearby parish for Mass at 12:30 p.m. About 20 years ago, St. Pope John Paul II made this church the National Sanctuary of Divine Mercy. It was so crowded that I couldn't get a seat anywhere. So I decided to concelebrate, which always gives a great seat. Unfortunately, the priest couldn't say Mass fast enough. After the Gospel, which was read in Italian (of course), another concelebrant proclaimed the Gospel in Polish. There was a large group of Polish pilgrims. This church is the National Shrine of Divine Mercy, which was made "famous" by the Polish nun, St. Faustina. The order of nuns that she belonged to serves in that church. I distributed communion, which is always a grace and a privilege. I love watching people come for communion. Pilgrims come from all over the world to this church. After Mass I was able to pray in front of the relics of St. Pope John Paul II and St. Faustina.

I went back to the hotel and, after a twenty-minute

nap (which turned out to be four hours long), I walked to a nearby restaurant for dinner. At one point I was certain that I had died and gone to heaven. Then I realized I was just eating gnocchi in a bolognese sauce with crusty Italian bread—totally delicious.

When I went to bed on that Sunday evening I reflected on two things:

(1) I will live and die as a Catholic. I love, love, love the Church, and I am so grateful for the faith that God has given to me. I am so grateful for the life of the Church. Even with all its faults and failings and sins and errors, I love the Church. It is in the Church that I find Jesus Christ, my Lord and Savior—the one who has saved me and is saving me, the one who has poured out his mercy on me, the one who is everything to me. I find Jesus alive in the Church, in the sacraments of the Church, in the people who make up the Church, in Pope Francis. I will live and die as a Catholic. I am so grateful for this faith handed on to me by my parents.

(2) I will always be fat. If carbohydrates are my downfall, let me fall! Italy is filled with bread and pasta. The crust on the bread is

totally delicious. I could just eat the crust. And the pasta is great. I can't get enough of either the bread or the pasta. When I went to bed each night, I could hardly wait for the morning so that I could have more bread. And that crust…I will always be fat. Sorry, Dr. Atkins. You have no currency with me.

Tuesday, February 9, was the day scheduled for the Holy Father to speak to the Missionaries of Mercy. I am told that 700 Missionaries have traveled to Rome for these days and to be sent forth by the Holy Father. We all assembled at the spot where the pilgrimages begin. It's about a quarter-mile walk to St. Peter's. There were 700 of us and we were divided into seven language groups—Italian, English, Spanish, French, German, Portuguese, and Polish. We walked together in pilgrimage, singing and praying psalms. It was beautiful. I saw one other priest that I knew from our ADELANTE Conference at Notre Dame some years ago. As we entered the Holy Door, I kissed the door and begged to be open to God's mercy (which I desperately need), and that I might be able to extend that mercy. We walked by the Tomb of St. Peter as well as the relics of St. Padre Pio of Pietrelcina and

St. Leopold Mandic. These relics were brought to the Vatican for just a few days. These two saints were renowned for being good and gentle confessors. They drew thousands and thousands of pilgrims. I am told that Padre Pio's body is intact, though it looks like he has had more facelifts than Phyllis Diller. It was very moving to see the bodies of these two holy men.

After going through the Basilica, we walked for what seemed like an hour to the *Sala Regia* in the Apostolic Palace. Once there, we climbed about 500 steps—give or take one! When we got to the *Sala Regia* I was able to find a seat in row 6. I was fairly close, but I wanted to get closer. After a short while, Archbishop Rino Fisichella, the President of the Pontifical Council for the Promotion of the New Evangelization, spoke to us about the talk that the Pope would give us and about the details of Mass on Ash Wednesday with the Holy Father. He reminded us to silence our cell phones!

At one point a priest in row 3 picked up his chair and moved to row 1, so I picked up my chair and moved to row 3. I was at the end of the row. I was sitting behind a priest who had his luggage next to him.

(I have no idea why—maybe he had the Sunday collection in it?!) I kindly asked him if he would mind putting his luggage to the side. He did and I moved up to row 2, where I sat immediately behind a priest in a wheelchair. From having watched the Holy Father on television many times, I knew that he always goes to people in wheelchairs first. I was hopeful. I thought about trying to find a stretcher!

While we were waiting I went up to the front and spoke with Archbishop Fisichella. I asked him if he knew if the Pope would greet priests in the front rows after his talk. He looked at me like I had two heads, shrugged his shoulders, rolled his eyes and said, "This is Francis. No one quite knows what he is going to do." I love Pope Francis.

At 5:30 p.m. the Holy Father arrived, though actually seeing him was preceded by lots and lots of clapping as he was walking in. Being in the second row, I was very close to him. His presence, his physical presence, is powerful. I kept thinking: "This is the Pope. I am so blessed and fortunate to be here." It is so easy to see his Italian features— he looks so Italian—and he talks with his hands.

He spoke in Italian. On the way into the *Sala Regia* we were given headphones and you could program them for different languages. During his talk I had the choice of listening to him in Italian and understanding about 80% of what he said, or of listening to a translation in English with headphones. I chose to listen to him in Italian. Part of the reason is that I love his voice. He has a beautiful, easy and soothing, voice.

In his talk he implored the Missionaries of Mercy to be gentle, to be kind, to be loving—to show the maternal face of the Church to penitents. He used this phrase a lot. "The Church is Mother because she nourishes the faith; and the Church is Mother because she offers God's forgiveness, regenerating a new life, the fruit of conversion." He asked us to reflect on our own sinfulness and on our own need for mercy, for forgiveness, and to extend that to all who come into the confessional. The Holy Father said, "We are His ministers; and we are always the first to be in need of being forgiven by Him."

He asked us to not be curious, to not be inquisitive, and to not ask questions that don't help the penitent at all. "Please," the Pope said, "this is not the good shepherd; this is the judge who perhaps believes he has not sinned, or the poor sick man who asks questions out of curiosity." He asked us to understand the language of gestures. He said, "You know when someone just can't say it...let them be. Their trying is enough. Their being there is enough. Use the language of gesture." Each time he said this, he would shrug his shoulders and use gestures. He said that the wise and holy confessors can understand and speak the language of gestures. He reminded us that, when people come to confession, they are feeling shame. And our role should be to say to them, with word and gesture, "It's okay. It's okay." This is how a real father treats his children. He kept insisting that the role of the confessor was to restore people to their dignity and begged us not to do anything that would work against that.

He referred, as he often has in his writings and speeches, to the time that he went to confession on September 21, 1953, as a teenage boy. "I have no idea what the priest told me. All I can remember is that the priest smiled and I felt so forgiven. This is what a father does. He encourages. He helps." The

Holy Father said, "If you can't smile, if you can't use the language of gestures, if you can't offer mercy and forgiveness, then don't hear confessions. Go and do something else."

At the end of his talk, the Holy Father told us, "Trust in the strength of mercy that comes to meet everyone as the love which knows no bounds. And say, like so many holy confessors: 'Lord, I forgive; put it on my account!'" This kind of comment makes me love the Pope more and more and more.

When he finished his talk he gave us the Apostolic blessing. Then he walked toward us. I was in the second row and I saw him coming right towards us. I couldn't believe it. And before I knew it, he was stretching out his hands into the crowd. I took his left hand, kissed it, put my cheek on it, and all I could say was *Santo Padre...Santo Padre...Santo Padre*. I had a few words prepared to say to him in Spanish. And I was going to give him a pair of those great Guadalupe socks for his upcoming trip to Mexico. But when I touched his hands, I couldn't say anything except *Santo Padre...Santo Padre...Santo Padre*. Being in his presence was enough. His hands are very soft. I didn't want to let go of his hands. This is a moment that I will never forget and will forever cherish. Well, I say that I will never forget it, but that night I kept asking myself, "Did that really happen?" I will be forever grateful. When the Holy Father walked out of the room, we all sang the "*Salve Regina.*" Now, I am no fan of Latin, but 700 priests from every corner of the globe singing together was powerful and beautiful. It's the only thing I know in Latin. And I was so glad to sing with all the other priests.

After the talk there was a dinner for the priests in the Paul VI hall. I met a few other Americans there. One priest came up to me and said, "Notre Dame, ACE, Latinos…" He had been at a talk I gave in Denver in October. It was a wonderful day, filled with grace and mercy. Tomorrow I will go to the General Audience with the Holy Father and then in the afternoon he will celebrate Mass and the Missionaries of Mercy will concelebrate with him. At some point during the Mass, he will give us the mandate to serve as Missionaries of Mercy.

When I walked from the Vatican to the hotel, I was thinking about having kissed the hand of Pope

Francis and having caught his glimpse for a moment, of what it was like to be in his presence and to listen to him and to watch him. And I can say this: he is exactly the person you see on television. He is himself. He is comfortable in his own skin. He exudes humility and mercy, both of which I need to grow in.

When I went to bed on Tuesday evening, I reflected on how I couldn't say anything to the Holy Father when he was in front of me. I just wanted to be in his presence. It made me think of what it will be like when we meet God—no words will be necessary. Just being in his presence will be enough.

On Ash Wednesday morning I went to the General Audience at the Vatican. The Pope looked and sounded tired. I wondered how he would have the strength for a very busy apostolic visit to Mexico, which was to start in two days. So I decided that one of the things that I would give up for Lent is to stop saying "I'm tired" even if I am. The Pope must be tired. Yet he never says, "I'm tired." He's 79 and has one lung. I thought to myself…if we really give ourselves over to the service of God and of the Gospel, we should be tired. Imagine giving yourself over to

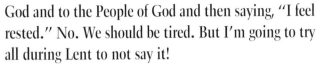

God and to the People of God and then saying, "I feel rested." No. We should be tired. But I'm going to try all during Lent to not say it!

The universality of the Church is so clear in General Audiences with the Holy Father. You hear lots of languages being spoken in the crowd. The Audience begins with a Scripture passage which is proclaimed in Italian by the Holy Father. Then priests proclaim the passage in English, French, German, Spanish, Portuguese, Polish, and Arabic. The Pope gives a brief homily in Italian and then those same priests give the translation. The Holy Father spoke about the Jubilee Year of Mercy and Lent. It's so clear that he wants everyone to experience the mercy of God. He is opening doors and hearts and lives everywhere.

After the Audience I went to the offices of *L'Osservatore Romano*, the Vatican newspaper. I had learned that you can check out all the pictures from the previous day there. So I found the pictures of me kissing the hand of the Holy Father. I bought a bunch of pictures—and I am so grateful to have these pictures. For one thing, I know that it actually happened!

Ash Wednesday Mass with the Holy Father was at

5:00 p.m. We had to arrive at 3:00 p.m. We vested and waited and talked and visited. I was struck by the commonalities of priests—all of us with our own versions of sin and grace across many cultures and languages trying to love God and be faithful priests in service of the People of God. I was very happy to be with the other Missionaries of Mercy.

We all processed into St. Peter's Basilica around 4:30 p.m. and Mass started at 5:00 p.m. It was a beautiful liturgy. The first reading was in English, the second reading was in Spanish, and the Gospel was in Italian. Most of the Mass was in Italian, though some was in Latin. I felt so privileged to be concelebrating Mass at St. Peter's where millions and millions of people from every corner of the world have come to pray for hundreds of years. I was so moved when one of the Cardinals put ashes on the head of Pope Francis. The Pope constantly reminds us that he, too, is a sinner. Still, seeing this moved me deeply. We all need to be forgiven. We all need the mercy of God.

I was struck several times during my days in Rome, and especially at the Mass, by how smart phones have united the world. During the Mass the priest on my left was from Prague. As the readings were being proclaimed, he was reading them in Czech on his iPhone. I saw a Polish priest and a priest from Germany doing the same thing. It's kind of amazing when you think about it—how cell phones have united the world. We all have them.

All during the day on Ash Wednesday I did not see anyone with ashes. I thought...does no one here go to Church on Ash Wednesday? Even cultural Catholics go on this day. I learned why at the Mass. In Italy, ashes are sprinkled on the top of your head. They are not put on your forehead like we do in the United States, so you don't see them.

After Communion, the Pope prayed a beautiful prayer sending out the Missionaries of Mercy to be the maternal face of the Church to all who come seeking the mercy of God. I was deeply moved by the prayer, but even more so by his gentle yet strong voice. I will treasure always the moment of being sent forth by the Holy Father. At the end of every talk and presentation by the Holy Father, he says: *"Non dimenticare di pregare per me"* ("Don't forget to pray for me"). He's very serious about that and such a great role model about asking for prayer.

My days in Rome were days of grace and mercy. They were filled with prayer and pasta, with blessings and bread. I leave Rome with a total desire to serve as a Missionary of Mercy. Please pray for me that God might use me to be the face of mercy for all who come seeking mercy and forgiveness.

Lord Jesus Christ, Son of the Living God,
have mercy on me, a sinner.

Being Mercy:
What Does a
Missionary of Mercy Do?

E ver since my appointment as a Missionary of Mercy I have received several hundred e-mails and notes and phone calls congratulating me, promising me prayers, and asking questions. Some of these were from students I taught at Notre Dame in the late 1970s and early 1980s when I was a seminarian and they are people I have not heard from since. It has been very humbling as well as touching and encouraging. Many people have spoken to me in person also.

Most people don't know quite what to say. The most common comment is: "Congratulations on your promotion." While people mean well, I know that this is not a promotion. And I'm certain that this was not in the mind of the Holy Father when he thought up the idea of the Missionaries of Mercy and then appointed us.

I tell people that all it takes to become a Missionary of Mercy is to be a big sinner and to repent constantly. In the seventh chapter of the Gospel of St. Luke, Jesus goes to the home of Simon for dinner. While there a woman stops by who washes the feet of Jesus with her tears and then dries them with her hair. Simon mumbles under his breath. Jesus says, "She has loved much because her many sins have been forgiven." Jesus says that she has sinned much, has been forgiven much, and now loves much. He seems to hint that there is a direct correlation between sin and the ability to love. What makes us love God more and more? When we are forgiven over and over? And so it is in life.

So to become a Missionary of Mercy, one needs the following: to be aware of the depth of one's sin; to know of one's lack of inner and outer resources to make much progress in overcoming sin; to want to stop sinning; and to rely incessantly on the mercy of God—and then to extend that mercy to others. That's the pattern.

Because of the limits of my humanity I am painfully aware of my sins. And at age 61, I am all too aware of my inability to make much progress in over-coming them. I will be getting social security soon, but that won't help me much in my struggle against sin. Because of God's faithfulness and tender love, I know a lot about His mercy and forgiveness. And I want to extend that mercy to everyone.

Students contact me very regularly asking for an appointment to talk with me about spiritual direction. And I always tell them: "This is what I bring to the table. I've been sinning for a lot longer than you have been, so I know way more about mercy and forgiveness than you do!"

So there you have it. That's the way it works. When I tell people that all it takes to be a Missionary of Mercy is to be a big sinner and to thereby know lots about God's mercy, they look at me kind of strangely. They somehow imagine that to have been appointed as a Missionary of Mercy you must have overcome sin. *Dios mío*—quite the opposite.

What is it about how we have come to think about life that everything is supposed to be an upgrade or a promotion or upward move? This is all backwards and upside down.

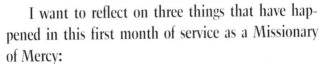

I want to reflect on three things that have happened in this first month of service as a Missionary of Mercy:

(1) I have met with lots and lots of people who want to talk with me or who want to go to confession. Some have imagined that I now have powers that allow me to regularize marriages outside of the Church and this sort of thing. That day might be coming, but is not here yet.

(2) I have been asked to lead and preside at local parish penance services and then to hear confessions.

(3) I have given retreats and days of recollection to priests.

A word on each…

Many people have called for appointments to go to confession or to seek answers or counsel in difficult situations. I am always edified by how many people who are in a second marriage (outside the Church) still love the Church and still want to be part of the Church. Most are seeking annulments. Their love for the Church and their desire for the Eucharist always invite me to not take the Eucharist for granted. All is a gift from God. When people come to confession, I am so aware that the person coming is trying, wants to do better, is embarrassed and often feels shame. I try as hard as I can to help them understand that what we have here is one sinner confessing to another sinner. I pray that I can smile at every person, and that every person will leave the confessional with trust in the relentless mercy of God, or at least wanting to trust in that mercy.

Parish penance services...I can't even count how many of those I led and how many of those I helped with in other parishes when I was the pastor of St. John Vianney in the Diocese of Phoenix for twelve years and then pastor of Holy Redeemer in the Archdiocese of Portland for seven years. They always bring God's salt-of-the-earth people wanting to go to confession: "I have been judgmental"; "I fight with my spouse"; "I gossip at work"; "I'm impatient with my children"; "I don't like my mother-in-law"; "I tell white lies"— good, honest people wanting to do better. I love parish penance services because, for the most part, there is no pretense—just straightforward confessing of sins—no dodging them, no explaining them away.

When I was a pastor I used to think that we needed to find ways to engage those who rarely or never come to Church who want to experience the mercy and forgiveness of God. What kind of prayer or gathering could we organize that would draw people who rarely or never come so that they also could know the relentless, inexhaustible mercy of God?

Preaching to priests is in a category all its own. I am in the middle of preaching a Lenten retreat at Holy Cross House on Notre Dame's campus to about 70 retired and ill Holy Cross priests and brothers. Just standing in front of some of the giants of the Holy Cross community is intimidating. Some of these men have been my Superiors. Some have taught me. Almost all know me. As I talk about mercy I look out and wonder which one of those guys I will be in 15–20 years. Will I be like Father X who has Parkinson's? Will I be like Father Y who can't stay awake? (I'm kind of like that now!) Will I be like Father Z who cannot accept that the aging process is winning in his life? Which one of those guys will I be?

After each talk I am available for confession. They

come in one by one. They are so honest about their lives. I am constantly humbled. They know themselves through and through. One said to me, "I wish that I could live my entire life over so that I could live my life from a perspective of mercy and forgiveness rather than a perspective of sin and judgment." "It's not too late," I say, "to receive the mercy and tender forgiveness of God. He wants you to have it. He's giving it to you."

I have also had the privilege of preaching days of recollection to all the priests in several dioceses. Again, this is a unique privilege—for one priest to stand in front of 100 priests and to talk about the mercy of God and then to be available for confessions afterwards. I am always humbled and moved. Sometimes I cry. "Father, it's okay. You are not perfect... and you're not required to be."

It is still unclear to me why I have been chosen to serve as a Missionary of Mercy. But then is anything about my life clear to me? I know that God is up to something. I pray every day for Him to transform me more and more into His Son. I am convinced that part of how God is doing this is through my hearing confessions and offering the mercy of God to all who come, freely given to us all the time.

Lord Jesus Christ, Son of the Living God,
have mercy on me, a sinner.

Being Mercy:
I Don't Always Say Thank You

When Pope Francis met with the Missionaries of Mercy on February 9, 2016, he asked us to make every effort to hear confessions during the Jubilee Year of Mercy, and especially during the Season of Lent. As I mentioned in a previous reflection, the relics of St. Padre Pio of Pietrelcina and St. Leopold Mandic were brought to the Vatican to be present at Mass on Ash Wednesday, February 10, 2016, when the Holy Father commissioned the Missionaries of Mercy. Both saints were known to be wise and holy confessors spending many hours a day hearing confessions.

I served as pastor of St. John Vianney Parish in Goodyear, Arizona, for 12 years (1990-2002). St. John Vianney, or the Cure of Ars as he is more commonly known throughout the world, was famous for hearing confessions for 10-12 hours a day—every day.

I cannot count how many penance services I took part in during my 19 years as pastor—12 as pastor of St. John Vianney in the Diocese of Phoenix and 7 as pastor of Holy Redeemer in the Archdiocese of Portland-in-Oregon.

During the Season of Lent, in addition to the singular grace of hearing the confessions of priests, I had the opportunity to lead penance services and to hear confessions in a number of parishes in the Diocese of Fort Wayne–South Bend and in the Basilica of the Sacred Heart on the campus of the University of Notre Dame.

Hearing confessions in parishes is always a moment of grace, for both the penitent and for the confessor. Grace always "flows" in both directions. Both the priest and the penitent are recipients of God's grace. Old people and young people, parents and children, married people and widows, engineers and construction workers, executives and employees, managers and cafeteria workers, people who last went to confession twenty days ago and people who last went to confession twenty years ago, and everyone else. Much of this is true at the Basilica as well since lots of people from South Bend and many visitors go to confession in the Basilica.

During Holy Week I heard confessions for about 15 hours. I tried to remember the advice of the Holy Father when he spoke to us on February 9. "When people come to confession, smile at them. If you can't smile, go do other work." I smiled a lot.

Confessions are a unique privilege and opportunity to extend the mercy of God, and often to people who think that they are unworthy of it. "God is greater than any sin we could ever commit," I say over and over. "Our sins just melt away in the face of God's inexhaustible mercy." "You are so much more than any wrong you have ever done." "God sees far beyond your sin."

As they come to confession, I try to remember the words that the Holy Father spoke to us on February 9. "Be gentle, be kind, be loving; show the maternal face of the Church to penitents. The Church is Mother because She nourishes the faith; and the Church is Mother because She offers God's forgiveness—regenerating a new life, the fruit of conversion."

Pope Francis asked us to reflect on our own

sinfulness and on our own need for mercy—for forgiveness—and to extend that to all who come into the confessional. He reminded us that we cannot run the risk of having a single penitent not perceive the maternal presence of the Church, which welcomes and loves each one. Should this perception fail, due to our rigidity, it would do serious harm to the Faith itself, because it would impede the penitent from feeling included in the Body of Christ. Moreover, it would greatly limit the penitent's sense of belonging to a community. "Instead," the Holy Father said, "we are called to be the living expression of the Church, which as Mother welcomes whosoever approaches Her, conscious that through the Church one is joined to Christ. Entering the confessional, let us always remember that it is Christ who welcomes, it is Christ who listens, it is Christ who forgives, and it is Christ who grants peace. We are His ministers; and we are always the first to be in need of being forgiven by Him."

When I was a Novice, our Novice Master, Father Nicholas Ayo, CSC, often said this: "If everyone set their life story to music, you would recognize the melody everywhere." So true, so true. In the end, our sins are very similar.

The confessions of children are especially beautiful. Often they are very funny. Years ago a boy came to his First Confession, sat down in front of me, and said, "#3, #8, and especially #4." I really didn't know what he meant. When I asked him what he meant, he replied, "Oh, the commandments that I have broken." Another time, a girl about 12 years old said, "I find my little brother to be insufferable." I thought to myself, "Where did she learn that word?" There are many times while hearing the confessions of children that I have to hold back my laughter. They are so beautiful, so innocent, so funny, so real.

Recently a middle-school student came to confession. He said, "I don't always say thank you. And I often do things and find other people to blame." I realized at that moment that I was sitting in front of a theologian or a mystic or a saint. I wanted to ask him, "Did you do a doctorate in sacramental theology at Notre Dame?"

"I don't always say thank you." Imagine what a different place the world would be if we always said thank you. Imagine what a different person I would be if I always said thank you, if I saw everything as a gift, if the word "entitlement" were erased from my thinking and vocabulary. I am reminded of the words from the Dominican priest Meister Eckhart who wrote, "If the only prayer that you ever say in your entire life is thank you, that will be enough."

"I often do things and find other people to blame." Again, imagine what a different world we would live in if we were not always looking to pass the blame on to someone else, if we were willing to own up to what we have done. It is really so freeing when I can say, "It was my fault. I did it."

Every time a priest hears confessions he is brought to be more honest with himself. Everything he hears makes him reflect on his own sinfulness and need for mercy. Often I hear someone confess something that I have given up struggling with. I am often indicted by other people's confessions. I have to ask myself, "When did I fail to say thank you?" Or "When I have done something wrong and tried to pass the blame to someone else?"

·I leave the confessional, stole in hand, so grateful to a merciful God who has shown me a lifetime of mercy and who has called me to serve Him and His

Church as a priest. What a privilege, what a grace, what a blessing to be able to extend that mercy to all who come seeking the mercy of a God whose name is mercy.

There is such beauty and grace and humanity and holiness in the sacrament of confession. I am so encouraged that this sacrament of mercy and forgiveness is making a comeback, so to speak, in the Church today. How could it not? For all of us constantly stand in need of mercy and forgiveness. And how blessed are we that "His mercy endures forever."

Lord Jesus Christ, Son of the Living God,
have mercy on me, a sinner.

Being Mercy:
The Parable of the Merciful Father

Pope Francis is not the first person to suggest that the parable that we all know as "The Parable of the Prodigal Son" is not named well. The Pope prefers to call this parable the "Parable of the Merciful Father." The parable is really about the mercy and forgiveness and love of the Father, not about the sons. This parable might well be considered the "Parable for the Year of Mercy."

The parable may well be the most well-known of the parables. Everyone knows the story. After talking with his father, the younger son takes his share of his father's inheritance, moves far away from home, squanders his money on loose living, gets hungry, and decides to go back home. He imagines that he is not worthy of the father but, at least, he can get a job as one of his father's servants.

He has carefully prepared what he will say to his father when he arrives home.

The older son has fulfilled every wish of his father, has done whatever he was asked to do, has always been loyal to the father. But when the father throws a party for his errant son, the older brother becomes angry. He does not want to be associated with the father. He does not want to come into the house.

When I graduated from Notre Dame in 1976, Dom Helder Camara, the then-archbishop of Olinda and Recife, Brazil, received an honorary doctorate. I was lucky enough to meet him, and I still have a picture of him and me on my desk in my office.

In reflecting on this parable the archbishop wrote, "I pray incessantly for the conversion of the older brother. The younger brother has awakened from his life of sin. When will the older brother awaken from his life of virtue?" I have never forgotten those words, and I have returned to them often over the past forty years.

The two sons have so much in common. Each son had his self-made plans for happiness. The older son was certain that if he obeyed all the laws, did what he was supposed to do, and always respected his father that this would make him happy, but it did not.

The younger son had his self-made plans for happiness. He lived a wild and crazy life, did what he wanted to do, spent money freely, and thought of his own needs first. He thought that this would make him happy, but it did not.

Both sons had their own self-made and self-designed plans for happiness. And neither plan worked.

Both sons are guilty of the same sin. The younger son thinks that he is too bad to receive the mercy of God. And the older son thinks that he is too good to need it. One doesn't deserve it. The other doesn't need it. Both think that they are responsible for their own salvation. But neither one is responsible for his salvation. The mercy of God will save both.

Neither son wants to go into the house. The older son is too angry to go into the house. And the younger son feels too "dirty" to go into the house. Both sons mistreat the father, yet the father takes neither one to task nor asks either one to repent. The father loves both sons and offers them his mercy.

The father goes out the front door of the house to welcome the younger son. The younger son has a speech all prepared about not being worthy to be his son and he is willing to work as a servant. The father does not let him finish his speech. Instead he interrupts him, asks nothing of him, hugs and kisses him, and offers him everything that he is. It is interesting to note that the father does not ask the son to bathe or wash or to cut his hair, or to put on clean clothing. Rather the father just puts everything on top of what the son already is wearing. God always meets us exactly where we are.

The same father goes out the back door of the house to talk with the older son who refuses to come into the house. He pleads with him and invites him to be compassionate by offering him his mercy. The father says to the older son: "Son, everything that I have is yours." When he says "everything that I have is yours," he does not mean the fattened calf, the ring, the robe, the slippers. What he means is that everything that he is—mercy, compassion, love, tenderness, goodness, forgiveness—is the son's as well.

The words that the father speaks to the older son

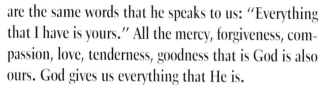

are the same words that he speaks to us: "Everything that I have is yours." All the mercy, forgiveness, compassion, love, tenderness, goodness that is God is also ours. God gives us everything that He is.

We do not know what either son does. We do not know if the younger son comes into the house through the front door or if the older son comes into the house through the back door. Both sons mistreat the father in the same way. And the father loves both sons as each one needs to be loved. You can easily see why a more correct name would indeed be "The Parable of the Merciful Father." My guess is that both sons eventually come into the house because the father's mercy is so strong that eventually they succumb to it.

This is how the Father is with us. It is His mercy that saves us. Our good works do not save us. Nor do our sins disqualify us. It is His infinite and tender and relentless mercy that reaches out to us and saves us. In the end we are all saved by the relentless, inexhaustible mercy of God.

Lord Jesus Christ, Son of the Living God,
have mercy on me, a sinner.

Being Mercy:
Reflections on a Trip to the Holy Land

I never had much interest in going to the Holy Land, primarily because I thought that it would never happen. Then one day last fall I was flying somewhere and doing e-mail on the plane, when an e-mail arrived about a trip to the Holy Land. I read it, was intrigued, and decided that I really wanted to go. So I submitted my name and was accepted to the trip. I will be eternally grateful.

Day 1: May 19

I flew out of the South Bend International Airport on Wednesday, May 18, in the afternoon—to Detroit, New York's JFK, and then from JFK to Tel Aviv. We landed in Tel Aviv around 5:10 p.m., May 19, and went through Immigration and Customs. It was much easier than many stories I had heard prior to the trip. Then I found an ATM and took out some shekels. This sounds kind of silly, but I keep laughing every time I think that I have shekels in my pocket! "Shekels" is such a funny word to me. We took a shuttle to Notre Dame's Ecumenical Institute in Tantur. Upon arriving in Tantur we had dinner, then time for a short rest, and then Mass. After Mass the group of pilgrims visited with each other.

Some first impressions: I cannot stop thinking of my mom (may her soul rest in peace) who was Syrian. Her parents were born in Aleppo, Syria, and immigrated to the United States in the mid-1920s. People here look like my mom. I hear them talking Arabic and so many sounds from childhood come back to me, especially the guttural sound that comes from somewhere deep in the throat. It almost sounds like the speaker is trying to clear his or her throat. I hear phrases and words and then other phrases and words from my childhood come back to me. How I wish I would have learned Arabic when I was a kid. When I meet people, they make me think of my mom. She was much more Syrian than I thought—and, as it turns out, so am I.

We had *sauseegio* for dinner. (I have no idea how to spell that word, but I remember that food so clearly from when Titah—my maternal grandmother—would make them.) They are thin little sausages and they are very good. They have great flavor. We also had *za'atar*. I have no idea what it is. You take a piece of Syrian bread (more commonly known here as pita bread), smear olive oil on it and then you put *za'atar* (a mixture of different seeds, I think) on it. We used to call that Syrian dirt. *Za'atar* is totally delicious.

Day 2: May 20

Today for our dessert at lunch they served those cookies that my Aunt Mary used to make called caa-ak. They were round and had anise in them. And at dinner tonight we had Syrian rice. Just from looking at it, I could tell it was what my mom would have called "Syrian rice." It was delicious.

After dinner we went to the Western Wall, also known as the "Wailing Wall." It is the only standing wall from the Temple that Jesus preached in when he was in Jerusalem. Thousands of people come to the Western Wall every day, but mostly on Friday night when the Sabbath is beginning. Most were Orthodox Jews coming to pray—very moving, very powerful. Before entering we washed our hands with jugs filled with water from a water fountain. I stopped to pause and think that Jesus did the same thing and in the same spot. As I got closer to the wall itself, I had to put on a white skull cap like Orthodox Jews wear. A guard motioned to me to tuck my Cross inside my shirt. I saved the white skull cap in case I'm ever elected Pope!!

I went to the wall and touched it and prayed for my family and friends. I prayed for peace. I kept touching the wall and running the palm of my hand on the wall. I kept asking Jesus to make me like him. All I kept thinking is that Jesus might have touched that very spot on the wall, but even if not, he preached in that temple. It was very, very moving.

Even though I went to the Western Wall as a pilgrim, not as a tourist, it's hard not to feel like an outsider going into someone's home or space to pray. I was deeply moved by the emotion of the Jewish people praying at the Wall—the chanting, the sobbing, the rocking, the praying—all of it was very moving indeed.

Day 3: May 21

Today we went to Bethlehem. First we went to Shepherd's Field...the field where the shepherds were tending their sheep when the Angels told them of the birth of Jesus. When you walk onto the field there is a big archway with the words *Gloria in Excelsis Deo*—beautiful. We celebrated Mass in an outdoor chapel. It was peaceful and calm and beautiful. We celebrated the Mass of Christmas Day and sang Christmas songs. On the one hand, it felt strange to be singing "Hark the Herald Angels Sing" and "Angels We Have Heard on High" on May 21; but, on the other hand, it was amazing to sing those songs in the field where the Angels first told the shepherds about the birth of Our Savior. After Mass I went into several caves where the shepherds would have stayed at night. There is a really beautiful Chapel in one of the caves. I walked in and people were singing "Angels We Have Heard on High." The "Gloria" refrain made me cry.

After that we had a TOTALLY DELICIOUS lunch. The people of the Middle East certainly know how to use spices to make things taste delicious! We had many different salads including the ever-present hummus. We had shish kebabs with lamb, beef, and chicken—so good. The taste reminded me of the *mischwe* (Arabic word for shish kebab) that we would have at my maternal grandparents' home every Sunday when we would go to visit them. I can still see the pot in which my grandmother used to prepare the *mischwe*. And there was lemonade with mint flavoring—to die for.

After lunch we went to the center of town, called Manger Square. First we went to the Church of the Milk Grotto. The story says that, while Joseph and Mary were fleeing to Egypt with Jesus, Mary was nursing Jesus and a drop of her breast milk fell to the ground. The ground and cave where this happened turned a whitish color and has been that way ever since. There is a spectacular painting of Mary nursing Jesus—one that you do not see often, if ever. I had never seen it before. Hundreds of people go to this Church to pray for Mary's intercession to conceive a child. Being there was very, very moving. I prayed for several couples that I know for whom God has not yet granted conception. If it be His will, may God grant them the blessing of conceiving a child.

And then we went to the Church of the Nativity. In this church is the spot where Christians believe that Jesus was born. Hundreds and hundreds of people go to this church in order to kneel down to touch and kiss the spot where Jesus was born. I will never forget what it felt like to kneel down and kiss and touch that spot where Our Lord was born. I just kept rubbing my hand on the spot. I am so thankful for the opportunity to have done this.

I rubbed the Western Wall. I rubbed the spot where Jesus was born. There was to be a lot of rubbing on this trip! I ask myself why? It's because I want whatever I am rubbing to get into me—the prayers and supplications and petitions of the Western Wall, and the spot where Jesus was born. Often when Pope Francis talks about mercy he moves his palm as though he were rubbing, massaging in the mercy of God. We all want that mercy massaged into us.

Bethlehem is very commercial with vendors selling their wares everywhere—mangers, oil, incense, flags, banners, rosaries, and a thousand more things. (My favorite is a sign that reads: "Make hummus, not walls!") On the one hand, it seems so strange to see people and vendors selling all sorts of things in this most sacred place; but it also reminds me of the juxtaposition of all sorts of things in this life. Seeming opposites are often side by side, such as grace and sin! In every person's life, there are lots of "opposites" that co-exist. In the same day I can be very generous to a stranger, and I can be mean and stingy to a friend. Maybe they are not opposites... maybe they are complementary. Perhaps grace and sin are not opposites—just as east is not opposite from west...for if I go west and you go east, we will eventually meet.

The older I get the more I see that "and" is the most important word in Catholic theology. The word "or" has led the Church into schisms and divisions. The word "and" has kept the Church together.

Jesus is God **and** man. The Kingdom of God is here **and** to come. Mary is Virgin **and** Mother. We are people of grace **and** people of sin. I always say that the older I get, the better I look in grey!

Day 4: May 22

There were many things on our agenda today, but the highlight of the day was celebrating Mass at an outdoor chapel just 20 yards from the Jordan River

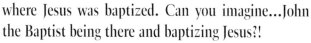

where Jesus was baptized. Can you imagine...John the Baptist being there and baptizing Jesus?!

We celebrated the Mass of the Lord's Baptism, and we all renewed our baptismal promises during Mass—very moving. After Mass we walked the 20 yards to the Jordan River. There were many people getting baptized in the water. I took off my sandals and walked into the water. The water is dirty and muddy. You'd think the river where Jesus was baptized would have clear and sparkling water—but no, dirty and muddy water. Maybe it's appropriate. Life is much more unclear than clear, more muddied than sparkling, more grey than black and white. My pants got wet, but they dried quickly in the desert heat. It's been very hot each day, and today's temperature was about 95° all day. It's a very dry heat and reminds me of Arizona.

The other highlight of the day was going to the City of Jericho. It's the oldest consistently inhabited city in the world. The city claims to be almost 12,000 years old and contains lots of interesting juxtapositions. Here was the oldest city in the world—ancient-looking buildings and ruins—with signs everywhere for Kentucky Fried Chicken, Snicker Bars and Sprite. We went to see the Sycamore tree that Zacchaeus climbed so that he could see Jesus when Jesus was walking through Jericho. To get there we drove on the road that most likely was the road Jesus refers to when he tells the parable of what has come to be known as the Good Samaritan.

Every so often I have to stop and pinch myself, thinking—am I really here? This is an amazing pilgrimage!

Tomorrow at 6:30 a.m., I will celebrate Mass in the Church of the Holy Sepulcher on the very spot where Jesus was nailed on the Cross. I am so grateful and so excited.

Day 5: May 23

Today is a day that I will never forget. We left Tantur at 5:30 a.m. and went to the Church of the Holy Sepulcher. From the earliest days, Christians revered and kept holy the sites where Jesus died on the cross, and where he was taken down from the cross, and where he was laid in the tomb, and the surrounding area. The Church of the Holy Sepulcher is built "on top of" all of these sacred sites.

As soon as you walk into the church, the first thing you see is a stone slab, believed to be where the body of Jesus was put after he died on the cross. The stone slab is about 1200 years old. So though it is not the same stone slab where the body of Jesus was laid, it's the same spot. As you might imagine, there is a lot of reverence around the stone. I knelt down and kissed the stone, and I prayed—asking forgiveness for all my sins and in gratitude to Jesus for dying on the cross for me so that all my sins would be washed away. I prayed to be open to his mercy so that I could be a more merciful person to myself and to others.

The stone had a beautiful smell to it. I learned that people come and anoint the stone with scented oils, like the women anointed the body of Jesus after he died. I knew that I would want to return to that spot later in the day when time permitted.

There is an altar and chapel on top of the spot where Jesus was nailed to the cross. It's called the Chapel of the 11th Station. I had the great honor and privilege of celebrating Mass for our pilgrimage group at that spot. All I kept thinking is that we are celebrating Mass on top of the very spot where Jesus was nailed to the cross. And just next to the altar, perhaps 15 feet west, is the spot where Jesus died on the cross. It is marked by a beautiful altar and lots of candles and other signs of reverence. The Mass was beautiful. I will be grateful to God forever for the opportunity to have celebrated Mass on this spot. As I write these words, I can still feel that moment.

After Mass we walked to see other places, including a Muslim mosque. From there we went to an area where it is believed that Mary was born and where her childhood home was. We sat outside and prayed. Then we went into a most beautiful church called the Church of St. Anne. There is a beautiful statue of St. Anne talking with her daughter Mary. It is tradition that every group that comes to the church is allowed to go to the front of the church and to sing a few hymns. The acoustics are incredible. Our group went to the front of the church and we sang "Hail Holy Queen," "Salve Regina," and the Notre Dame Alma Mater—totally beautiful and moving.

Then after that we went to see the remains of the pool of Bethesda where Jesus performed some miracles, including the man who told Jesus that "every time the water is stirred, I have no one to lift me up and put me in the water."

From there we walked a long portion of the *Via Dolorosa*, the Way of the Cross. We first stopped at the place known as *Ecce Homo*. This is where Pilate sentenced Jesus to death. You can see what is believed to be the bench that Pilate sat on when he sentenced Jesus to die. It is all very moving.

Then we walked the Way of the Cross. Every so often you will see a Roman numeral, which denotes a certain station. For example, "V" marks the fifth station. And there will be an inscription as to what that station is. There are shops and stores, and ATM machines, and kids running, and people selling food and drink all along the way. At first I was expecting to find the *Via Dolorosa* quiet and serene, and prayerful, and stark and lonely. It is the exact opposite, totally different. It is loud and noisy, and messy, and filled with people. But that is how it would have been when Jesus walked that path many years ago. There would have been people buying and selling and trading and making deals, kids running and playing and yelling, teenagers laughing and whispering, and so on. It's all very real. It makes you realize in a profound way that Our Lord was human and walked the same earth that you and I walk, and that he entered fully into this world and life and everything else. It is extremely powerful, but in a different way than you would think at first. It's as real as anything that I have ever seen.

While walking the Way of the Cross, I had a glass of freshly squeezed orange juice and then we stopped for lunch. We had three things that I could eat every day for the rest of my life: Syrian bread (pita bread), hummus, and falafel. What more do you need?!? It was delicious.

After lunch the group went to visit another site, but I went back to the Church of the Holy Sepulcher. On the way I went to an ATM to get some shekels and bought some olive wood rosaries. I also bought a small jar of anointing oil.

I went to the stone slab where the body of Jesus was laid after he was taken down from the cross. I knelt and prayed, and then I poured a few drops of the bottle of oil over the stone; and I gently spread the oil with my hands, and then my hankie, imagining that I was anointing the body of Jesus. And then I remembered the woman in the Gospel, and I poured the entire bottle onto the stone. It was so prayerful.

There is never a moment when people are not all around the stone doing the same thing—anointing the stone, kissing the stone, rubbing the stone, praying. I kissed the stone many times, and put my forehead on it, and prayed and cried. I took all the rosaries I bought and rubbed them on the stone.

Then I went up to the chapel where I had celebrated Mass in the morning. I also went to the altar just 15 feet west of where I had said Mass. There are hundreds of people in line. That's the spot that is revered as the spot where Jesus died. I knelt down and touched the spot. My heart was filled with gratitude to Our Lord for all that he has done for me. I will never be able to be grateful enough for his mercy poured out into my life, moment by moment, all my life long.

Day 6: May 24

I am fond of saying that the older I get the better I look in grey. The world, which seemed so black and white to me in my 20s and 30s, seems so much greyer to me at age 61. I think that, at some level, we prefer to live in a black and white world because it's easier and more clear cut, but that world does not really exist. The contrasts and paradoxes in the Holy Land are so obvious and remind us that a black and white world does not exist.

The Church of the Holy Sepulcher is shared by Orthodox Christians and Catholic Christians and a few other Christian groups. These groups do not get along and they do not trust each other. They fight often. I am told that a Muslim has the key to the Church and is in charge of the building. So none of the Christians trust each other, but they will trust the Muslim.

When I go to the sacristy at 6:20 a.m. to get ready to celebrate Mass—the Mass which is understood to be "outside of time" so to speak—I am told kindly, but sternly, by a young Franciscan priest who works in the sacristy: "25 minutes for Mass, Father. No longer, please! There's another Mass at 7:00 a.m."

When I walk out of the restaurant on the *Via Dolorosa* almost overdosing on falafel, I look up and see the "V" station marker on a wall: that this is where Simon of Cyrene offered to help Jesus carry his cross.

I could write for pages about the paradoxes and seeming opposites that I have seen here. And yet, what is the Paschal Mystery in the end? That dying is rising. Try making sense of that in your own life if you want to live in a black and white world—and for that matter, what of the Incarnation itself? Yet another paradox—that the maker of humanity would become human, that the one who existed from before time would be born into time, that the giver of Baptism would ask to be baptized, that the only One who can quench our thirst would ask the woman at the well for some water to drink...and so much more. Being in the Holy Land these days has affirmed what I have come to believe in my own life—the older I get, the better I look in grey.

Today we visited six churches and holy spots and took time to pray at each one. I mentioned earlier that since the beginning Christians have kept sacred the sites and places where very significant things have happened in the life of Jesus. St. Helena, the mother of Constantine, came to the Holy Land in 326 and for two years went about finding all the sites that Christians revered and kept holy. She saw to it that churches and chapels and shrines were erected on those holy sites.

(1) We first visited the church which commemorates where Jesus mounted a donkey to ride into Jerusalem as his passion was about to begin—a beautiful church. Each year the Catholics in Jerusalem begin Palm Sunday Mass on this spot.

(2) Then we visited the Church of the Pater Noster. This commemorates the spot where Jesus taught his apostles to pray the Our Father. This is a beautiful place where cloistered Carmelite nuns have a convent. The Our Father is written in calligraphy in large letters on beautiful ceramic tiles and walls in 174 languages, each one more beautiful than the next, and displayed all around the gardens. The entire area is so beautiful and prayerful. We prayed the Our Father at this site.

(3) We celebrated Mass at the church called *Dominus Flevit*, which means "The Lord wept." This recalls the site where Jesus wept over Jerusalem. There is the most beautiful panoramic view of Jerusalem from this site. There was a man there giving brief rides on a camel. Unfortunately, we didn't have time. I was so disappointed because I was dying to ride that camel! The camel, however, may have

been very glad that I wasn't able to ride him. I'm a lot heavier than all the kids getting camel rides!

(4) We visited the Basilica of the Agony in the Garden of Gethsemane. This basilica commemorates where Jesus prayed that he might not undergo his impending suffering, but in the end "your will be done, Father, not mine...." This church is so beautiful. I could have stayed there hours wanting to keep watch with the Lord, but like his apostles I probably would have fallen asleep!

(5) We visited the church called St. Peter in Gallicantu. This commemorates the spot where Peter denied Jesus three times. There is a beautiful—really beautiful—sculpture that shows Peter in the middle and he is surrounded by the three people who asked him if he knew Jesus, which he denied three times.

(6) We visited the Church of the Ascension. This commemorates the site from which Jesus ascended into heaven 40 days after his Resurrection. It is a beautiful church still owned by the Muslims. They let Christians visit it for an entrance fee. There is a footprint that has been molded into clay that claims to be the last footprint of Jesus before he ascended to

heaven. Many will say that it cannot be proven that it is the actual footprint of Jesus. The fact that, for 2000 years, millions of people have gone to that spot and have knelt down and have kissed that footprint makes it very real to me. I'm grateful to be one of those millions of people. As the Japanese novelist Shusaku Endo writes in his book *A Life of Jesus*: "Something does not have to be a fact for it to be true." I read that years ago and I have never forgotten it.

Today was a beautiful day, beginning at the Mount of Olives and tracing the footsteps of Jesus from what we call Palm Sunday to the Agony in the Garden...and then to the site from which he ascended into heaven.

Day 7: May 25

Today we took a bus ride to Nazareth. It's just over two hours from Jerusalem. It gave me a sense of how far Joseph and Mary came when they had to travel to Bethlehem at the order of Caesar Augustus when he ordered a census of the whole world. In those days it had to be a 3-5 day trip each way.

In Nazareth, the restaurant we went to for lunch

advertises that they serve what a first-century Jew living in Nazareth would have eaten for lunch. We had a wonderful meal: lentil soup, hummus and Syrian bread, a cabbage salad, olives, chicken and, for dessert, cut-up apples dipped in a date paste with honey. The meal was really delicious.

After lunch we went to the Basilica of the Annunciation, which is built on the spot where tradition believes that the Angel Gabriel came to Mary and asked her to be the mother of Jesus. The basilica is beautiful and it is the biggest church in the Middle East. We celebrated Mass using the readings and prayers from the Solemnity of the Annunciation. At the Creed, I bowed, as is always done, at the words, "and by the Holy Spirit was incarnate of the Virgin Mary, and became man." I bowed very profoundly as I was so aware of being in this holy place.

There is a small shrine in the church that marks the spot where the Angel Gabriel spoke to Mary. The Latin inscription translates to read: "The Word Was Made Flesh Here." I could not stop looking at that shrine—and the word "Here." How many hundreds of times I have prayed "And the Word Was

Made Flesh" in the Angelus! But Here! The Word Was Made Flesh Here! In this very spot, the Angel spoke to Mary and asked her to become the Mother of Jesus. It was extremely moving to be there and to pray in that exact spot. Here.

There is a much smaller church on the same property called St. Joseph's Church. There are beautiful statues and stained-glass windows of the foster-father of Jesus.

After Mass we drove to Tiberias. We are staying overnight at a kind of hotel there. It is right on the Sea of Galilee. This hotel is only for pilgrims visiting the Holy Land. It used to be owned by the Sisters of the Holy Cross. I can look out of my room and see the Sea. How incredible is that! And it is really beautiful. Tomorrow we will go for a boat ride on the Sea of Galilee.

As I look out at the Sea of Galilee I imagine Jesus on a boat talking with his apostles. I imagine Jesus and his followers hauling in the 153 fish from their catch. I imagine Jesus on the shore cooking breakfast for his followers. Just to think that Jesus lived here and walked these roads...I am so grateful to be here.

Day 8: May 26

We left Tiberias early this morning and made many stops. Our first stop was in the very north of Israel at Caesarea Philippi where Jesus asks his disciples who do people say that he is? After a few responses, he asks them, "Who do you say that I am?" Simon Peter confesses that Jesus is the Lord, the Son of God. And Jesus calls him "Peter" and tells him that he will be the rock upon which Jesus will build his Church. I wish that you could see the rock that Jesus might have been referring to. It is ENORMOUS!

After Caesarea Philippi, we went to Capharnaum. As you walk into the town, there is a big sign that reads, "Welcome to Capharnaum—the hometown of Jesus." This is where Jesus meets Peter for the first time. And the town is right on the Sea of Galilee. It's so easy to see why Jesus' followers were fishermen. Archeologists and historians are positive that a certain structure is the home of Peter's mother-in-law. It's only part of a home since it was discovered through excavation. There is a beautiful church built "on top of" the home. When you go into the church, there is a big glass window on the floor in the middle of the church. You can look through that window to see the house. It's amazing just to think that Jesus slept in that house! In Capharnaum there are also the remnants of the synagogue that Jesus preached in regularly and where he cured many people. For example, this is where he cured the man with a withered hand.

From there we went to the spot where Jesus multiplied the loaves and fishes. There is a really beautiful church there commemorating the spot. At the front of the church there is a stone discovered in the fourth century that has a loaf and a fish engraved into the stone. I sat there and prayed for some time, asking Jesus to take my loaves and fishes and to multiply them for the good of the Church and the world. And I thanked him for the gift of bread. I love bread!!

From there we went to the spot on the shore of the Sea of Galilee where Jesus prepared fish for the disciples after he rose from the dead. It is also the spot where Jesus asks Peter three times if he loves him. It is known as the Primacy of Peter. Again, there is a beautiful church on this site.

After visiting these four sites, we ate lunch at a

restaurant called Peter's Fish! What a great name for a restaurant! We had a delicious lunch and the main entree was Tilapia. It was very good.

After lunch we went for a one-hour boat ride on the Sea of Galilee. It was really beautiful. Many of us were hoping to jump from the boat and swim to shore as Peter did. But it was too windy and they would not let us do it. It seems like Risk Management has found its way to the Sea of Galilee!

After our boat ride, the bus took us to what is called the "Mount of Beatitudes" where Jesus preached what we know as the Sermon on the Mount. We are staying at a guest house of the Franciscan Sisters. It is totally beautiful, really beautiful. I tried to get Marriott reward points at the front desk since it's as nice if not nicer than any Marriott I have ever stayed in!

We celebrated Mass outside in a pavilion. We listened to both Matthew's and Luke's account of the Beatitudes. It is so amazing to listen to Gospel accounts where they happened!

We have done this at every site that we have visited. It is very moving to hear the Gospel account proclaimed at the spot, or near the spot, where the event actually took place.

How do we know that such and such event actually occurred at that spot? There are two ways. One is that, as I have said before, the earliest Christians kept sacred and revered the places and sites that were important in the life of Jesus—where he was born, where he lived, where he performed miracles, where he met Peter, where he taught, where he died, etc.

The other way is through excavation, whereby archeologists and historians have often uncovered remnants of structures or stones or materials that match what the early Christians have believed to be sacred sites.

We will spend the night tonight in the Mount of Beatitudes. And tomorrow we will go to Mt. Tabor where the Transfiguration took place.

Day 9: May 27

Today was a relatively easy day. After breakfast we went to Mt. Tabor. This is a very high mountain—and very steep. No wonder Jesus and his apostles were so skinny! My new title for Jesus is: Jesus, the

Mountain Climber! At what is a very high point, you can take a taxi from there to the top. It is really high up there—562 meters above sea level. I was having a hard time imagining Jesus and three of his apostles walking to the top of Mt. Tabor. This is where Jesus was transfigured before Peter, James, and John. Once on the top, it is really beautiful up there. Again, I am in awe when I think that, on this very mountain, Jesus was transfigured and was revealed to his followers as the Son of God. It is beautiful on the mountain and clear and gorgeous. We celebrated Mass in one of the chapels. Again, it's amazing to celebrate the feast of the Transfiguration on the very mountain top where Jesus was transfigured.

In the afternoon the bus took us to the town of Caesarea. It is in this town that Paul met Cornelius and it was revealed to him that the Gospel message was meant for everyone, not just the Jews. Caesarea is right on the Mediterranean Sea. The Mediterranean is beautiful and gorgeous. It was from here that Paul set out on many of his trips to bring the Gospel to faraway lands. After our stop in Caesarea, the bus took us back to Tantur.

Day 10 in Israel: May 28

Today the group went to Masada, an important place in Jewish history. I decided not to go because I wanted a day alone and I wanted to go back and see a few places that we had already seen. I wanted to buy a few things.

I walked from Tantur to the Bethlehem checkpoint. I went through the checkpoint and into Bethlehem. Then I took a taxi to Manger Square. I went to the Church of the Nativity, which contains the "spot" where Jesus was born. It was just a little after 8:00 a.m., and so it was not crowded yet. I was able to go and pray again in front of the spot where Our Lord was born—such a beautiful, sacred and holy spot. I knelt down, rubbed my hand on the spot and kissed the spot. I prayed asking Jesus to be born in me more and more. Then I walked to the Church of the Milk Grotto. It is a beautiful church, and I wanted to spend some time in prayer there also.

Then I took a taxi back to the checkpoint and I crossed back into Jerusalem. I took a taxi to the Jaffa gate. I then walked to the Church of the Holy

Sepulcher. I had been so taken by this church on Monday morning and afternoon that I wanted to return one more time. So I did. I was able to visit the actual tomb that Jesus was laid in after he died. There are three very sacred sites in that church—the place where Jesus died, the place where his body was laid after he was taken down from the cross, and the tomb. I had not gone to the tomb on Monday. There was a very long line of people waiting to go to the tomb. Finally it came my turn to go in. What can I say? You go into a beautiful ornate structure that was built to "encase" the tomb. But once inside—only four people at a time—you can see that it was a tomb in which a body could be placed. I kissed the tomb and prayed in thanksgiving for all that Jesus did to set me free and asked him to make me more grateful for that freedom. You can only stay for about a minute since there are so many people in line.

There is a stout Orthodox monk (who looks like he could be a cage fighter when he is not on duty at the tomb) moving everyone in and out. You would not want to cross him or get out of line.

From there I went to the stone slab where the body of Jesus had been placed after he was taken down from the cross. As on Monday, I knelt down and kissed the stone and touched my forehead to the stone. I love it there—I didn't want to leave that spot.

Then I went back to the spot on Calvary where the cross was and where Jesus died. The line was very short, and so within five minutes I had a chance to kneel down and kiss the spot where the cross was. I kissed it and touched it and prayed, "Lord Jesus Christ, Son of the Living God, have mercy on me, a sinner." I love that prayer.

Then I went to do some shopping. I bought a new suitcase to hold all the souvenirs that I have bought along the way! I also bought a few other items. As I was walking towards the Jaffa gate to look for a taxi, I could smell delicious hot baked bread. It was Syrian bread smothered with *za'atar*. It was really delicious. I could have eaten ten of them! Then I took a taxi back to Tantur.

So my time in Israel is coming to an end. Tomorrow I will fly to Rome. My pilgrimage to Jerusalem has been a remarkable and amazing gift to me. I will always be grateful for this opportunity. It's too early to say what this pilgrimage will mean to me over the next couple of months and years, but I can say this—I do not believe in Jesus any more now than when I started the pilgrimage. But seeing where he lived, walking in his footsteps, visiting so many holy sites—all this has made me want to know Jesus more and more. I know that I will read the Gospels with a fresh eye and ear. When I hear words and phrases like "Jericho," "Mt. Tabor," "the loaves and fishes," "Simon, do you love me more than these?" "the shepherds who were tending their flocks" and dozens more—I will listen more attentively, more closely. One thing I know for sure: Now that I have been to the Holy Land, I want to know Jesus better. And in knowing him better, I will want to love him more. And in loving him more, I will want to live more like him, to be transformed into him.

Oh dear God, please grant this prayer: Please transform me more and more into your Son.

Lord Jesus Christ, Son of the Living God,
have mercy on me, a sinner.

Being Mercy:
Hearing the Confessions
of the Confessors

Sometime last fall I received an e-mail about a pilgrimage to the Holy Land sponsored by the John S. Marten Program in Homiletics and Liturgics at Notre Dame. I had never been to the Holy Land, and I really did not have too much interest in going. I just imagined that I would never get there. I applied to go on the trip and was accepted. One of the other priests, Fr. Mike Connors, CSC, a dear friend and ordination classmate asked me, "Would you be willing to go to Rome for a few days after our trip to the Holy Land? I have never been to Rome and I'd love to go." There is always a good reason to go to Rome, so I told Mike that I'd be glad to go to Rome with him.

Each month during the Jubilee Year of Mercy the Holy Father reaches out to a different group of people. Little did I know when I said yes to Mike's invitation to go to Rome that our dates would partly coincide with a retreat that the Holy Father was planning to give to priests and seminarians around the world. June was the month for priests and seminarians. I only learned this by looking at the Jubilee website—im.va one day. I quickly registered for the retreat. It was to take place over a three-day period.

* * * * *

The first day, Wednesday, June 1, would be the Adoration of the Blessed Sacrament in designated jubilee churches in Rome with the opportunity for sacramental confession. This would be followed by catechesis and Mass by language groups. The second day, Thursday, June 2, would be the heart of the retreat. The Holy Father would preach three conferences to all the priests and seminarians who came to Rome for the retreat and to the rest of the world through Vatican Television. And the final day, Friday, June 3, the Feast of the Sacred Heart of Jesus, the Holy Father would preside and preach at Mass in St. Peter's Square. All the priests making the retreat were invited to concelebrate.

After registering for the retreat, I received an email asking me if I would be willing to be a confessor on the first day of the retreat. The Holy Father was asking any Missionary of Mercy who would be in Rome on June 1 to serve as a confessor in one of the Jubilee churches. I agreed to do so, of course.

I was assigned to a church known to Italians and tourists alike as *Chiesa Nuova*, which is located on Corso Vittorio Emanuele. The real name for *Chiesa Nuova* is *Santa Maria* in *Vallicella*. I don't think that anyone—including the pastor—knows it by this name! It is the church where St. Phillip Neri is buried. The church is a five-minute walk from Piazza Navona. Like dozens of other churches in Europe, the church is amazingly beautiful.

I went to the church around 1:30 p.m. to pray, and then I heard the confessions of priests from 2:00 to 4:30 p.m. The Jubilee volunteers put a sign on "my" confessional that read "ENGLISH / ESPAÑOL." The most difficult part of the afternoon was figuring out how to get inside the confessional! The confessionals in Italy are constructed differently than they are in churches in the United States. The "box" is a free-standing structure. I couldn't figure out how to open the little door/gate so that I could get inside the confessional and sit on the bench. I couldn't find the latch or the hook. I thought that I was going to have to jump inside the box! I finally found it, opened the door/gate and sat down. And there are all sorts of wooden flaps, so I spent the first ten minutes trying to figure it all out—and laughing at myself!

Then the priests began to come for confession in English and in Spanish. I could tell that most of the English-speaking priests were from Africa and Asia; and, because of their particular accents, the Spanish-speaking priests were from several different Latin American countries. All were in Rome for the Jubilee for priests.

* * * * *

The sins of priests are the same the world over. We take advantage of our position as priests and sometimes feel entitled. We gossip about parishioners to other parishioners. We tell white lies to make ourselves look better. We worry about crossing boundaries with staff or parishioners. We try to live a celibate life, which is not easy.

I could tell from listening to the priests going to confession, one after the next, that they so desperately want to believe what they tell penitents who come to them about God's mercy and God's forgiveness: that God forgives all, that God constantly shows us his mercy, and that God is filled with compassion and love for us.

As I thought about it, I realized that priests do believe what they tell penitents about the mercy and forgiveness of God. It's just that we also need to hear someone say it to us. I am so grateful that I could be the person telling priest after priest that God forgives, that God is merciful, that with our God there is mercy and fullness of redemption, that their sins are forgiven. And I'm very grateful for my confessor here at Notre Dame who also tells me that God forgives, that God is merciful, that God wants to show me mercy and forgiveness.

After confessions, later that evening, I thought of this analogy: Just like you cannot tickle yourself, you cannot tell yourself about God's mercy and forgiveness. Though we believe it, priests cannot tell themselves what they tell penitents every time they hear confessions. Well, we can, but it sounds so much better when someone else says it to us.

On Thursday, the first conference that the Holy Father gave was entitled "From Estrangement to Celebration." In his opening remarks he said this: "In our serene prayer, which wavers between embarrassment and dignity, dignity and embarrassment, let us ask for the grace to sense that mercy as giving meaning to our entire life, the grace to feel how the heart of the Father beats as one with our own." We certainly go back and forth from embarrassment to dignity and from dignity to embarrassment. Pope Francis continued: "We are at one and the same time sinners pardoned and sinners restored to dignity." Kind of my way of saying, 'I am a sinner whose sins are forgiven.'

The Holy Father told us priests, "This is how we have to see ourselves: poised between our utter shame and our sublime dignity. Dirty, impure, mean and selfish, yet at the same time, with feet washed, called and chosen to distribute the Lord's multiplied loaves, blessed by our people, loved and cared for. Only mercy makes this situation bearable. Without it, either we believe in our own righteousness like the

Pharisees, or we shrink back like those who feel unworthy. In either case, our hearts grow hardened."

What an extraordinary grace it is to be able to hear the confessions of priests, to feel one with them, to be one with them, to know of my own struggles to fully believe what I tell penitents every time I am privileged to hear someone's confession, and to help other priests truly believe that what we tell penitents is exactly the truth. Even though we have to live in the tension of sinners pardoned and sinners restored to dignity, between our utter shame and sublime dignity, we come to know that it is mercy—only God's mercy—that makes it all possible.

Lord, Jesus Christ, Son of the Living God, have mercy on me, a sinner.

*Lord Jesus Christ, Son of the Living God,
have mercy on me, a sinner.*

Being Mercy:
Mercy and Perfection

Earlier today, quite by chance, I saw another Missionary of Mercy. He was here at Notre Dame leading a workshop on spiritual direction. I remembered meeting him in Rome on February 9 and 10, when Pope Francis addressed the Missionaries of Mercy and then sent us forth to preach and proclaim and extend the mercy of God in whatever ways we could. I was standing behind him in line as we walked into St. Peter's Basilica. He had a Notre Dame backpack. I asked him if he worked at Notre Dame, and he explained that he has come to Notre Dame for several summers to lead workshops. And here he was at Notre Dame today!

We talked a little bit about the incredible grace and privilege that it has been to serve the Church as Missionaries of Mercy during this Jubilee Year of Mercy. He said, "I'm thinking of writing a letter to the Holy Father to thank him for this incredible year of mercy and to ask him to extend it for another year. It just can't end." I said, "I'll sign the letter also."

We both recognized that this Jubilee Year of Mercy has been a tremendous gift and blessing from God—and people don't want it to end. Of course, the mercy of God is relentless and it never ends; it will accompany us into eternity. But it might be a good idea to extend it! I said, "We've had enough Missionaries of Harsh Judgment for many years. We ought to have Missionaries of Mercy for many years also. We have gotten it wrong for so long that it can't be turned around in one year."

What have we gotten wrong? We think that we are saved when we get it right, when we stop sinning, when we become perfect. But the exact opposite is the truth. God saves us through our sins, through our imperfections, through our faults, through our failings, through our weaknesses. God saves us as sinners, not as saints.

For too many years we have failed to understand that the Good News is good precisely because mistake, failure, and sin are all part of what redeems us. We often say that we learn more from our mistakes than from our successes, but do we really believe this?

The great English mystic, Julian of Norwich, wrote: "First there is the fall, and then we recover from the fall. Both are the mercy of God." Read that again! Even the fall is the mercy of God. How wonderful is this! Most people are familiar with this line from Julian of Norwich's writings: "All will be well and all shall be well and all manner of things shall be well." But people have left off the first part of the sentence that puts it all in perspective. What Julian actually wrote is: "Sin is necessary…and all will be well, and all shall be well, and all manner of things shall be well." That line brings this sinner so much hope. I think that this part of the sentence has been consistently left out because people really don't believe it—yet it is what Julian wrote. The fall is the mercy of God. And so is the recovery.

We have completely misunderstood what Jesus means by perfection in the Gospel. We have taken it to mean what the word means in common parlance. Perfection means being perfect. But how can Jesus mean this? We know that only God is perfect. So how can we be perfect? If being perfect means making no mistakes and being without sin, then this is not possible. I'm not even sure I want it, at least in this life. Fr. Richard Rohr, OFM, writes: "The only perfection available to us humans is the ability to include and forgive our imperfections." We find this so hard to believe. Sometimes we don't even want to believe it. Yet this is precisely how God loves us. God loves us as he includes and forgives our imperfections and sins. What else can we mean when we say that God loves us exactly as we are? In recent years I've become fond of saying, "I'm not perfect, and I'm not required to be!"

We grow spiritually much more by doing it wrong than by getting it right. The phrase "Best Practices" has won the day. You hear it everywhere—classrooms, seminars, workshops, conferences, businesses. I think it's silly. When I give workshops and presentations, I always talk about "Worst Practices." We learn a lot more from our "worst practices" than from our "best practices." It's our worst practices that are our best teachers, just like our faults and failings and sins are our best teachers.

Just imagine what would happen if I began to believe that God loves me by including and forgiving my imperfections." If I believe this about myself, then I would have to start believing that this is how God loves everyone. Yikes! I would certainly be less tempted to be a "Missionary of Harsh Judgment" and more inclined to be a "Missionary of Mercy."

If you watch the Holy Father closely, and not even all *that* closely, it is so clear that this is what he wants us to grasp, to accept, to believe, to hold onto. The mercy of God is bigger than anything else. The mercy of God is relentless and free and available and accessible to everyone. And you cannot earn it. It's not about merit; it's about accepting who God is and how God gives himself to us.

Whether the Jubilee Year of Mercy is extended or not, Pope Francis hopes that we will make being merciful a way of life. The teaching of Thérèse of Lisieux can help us make mercy a way of life if we can believe what she taught—that "everything is a grace." That means that the fall is grace and the recovery from the fall is grace. Both are the mercy of God. Everything is a grace—everything!

Lord Jesus Christ, Son of the Living God,
have mercy on me, a sinner.

Being Mercy:
God's Non-Stop Mercy

L et me tell you a story…There is a local judge who is supposed to decide a complicated insurance case. The plaintiff, a widow, who is destitute, sends him two or three letters a day, makes innumerable phone calls, leaves endless voice mails, e-mails him every hour, sends dozens of faxes, texts him, begins a Facebook page, and has her friends calling in daily to recommend her cause and demanding justice for her. When the judge tries to leave his home or the court-house, she accosts him. She plants people in his path who give him messages about the widow. Sir, please help this poor woman. Listen to her case.

Finally, after several weeks of this treatment, the judge cannot stand the constant nagging anymore and, without even considering the merits of the case, decides to give her all that she wants.

Does this story sound familiar to you? It should because it's basically the parable from St. Luke's Gospel known as the Parable of the Unjust Judge and the Widow.

Here's the parable: "In a certain town there was a judge who neither feared God nor respected any human being. And a widow in that town used to come to him and say, 'Render a just decision for me against my adversary.' For a long time the judge was unwilling, but eventually he thought, 'While it is true that I neither fear God nor respect any human being, because this widow keeps bothering me I shall deliver a just decision for her lest she finally come and strike me.'"

Look at the parable more closely. We don't know anything about the widow. She is not presented as virtuous or even having a just cause. The judge is obviously not impartial or objective. So how can the Kingdom of God be similar to anything in this rather bizarre situation?

If a judge were a professional crook, it would not be so bad, but a judge is supposed to be a decent person who renders justice to people. The fact is that this judge is a wretched man—but the widow keeps knocking.

At the end of the parable, as Jesus is so good at doing, he leaves his listeners scratching their heads. What is this parable all about?

In all the parables, the listeners are to identify with someone. With whom can the listeners identify in this parable? Nobody wants to see himself or herself as the unjust judge. So who can the unjust judge be? I have heard too many homilies where God is somehow compared to the unjust judge and you, the person praying, are the widow. Maybe it's never said quite so explicitly, but the widow is always the one praying. So the unjust judge must be God. What an insult to God to think of God as the unjust judge! *Dios mío.* As Voltaire once wrote, "In the beginning God created man in His own image, and man has been trying to repay the favor ever since."

Since the parables are mirrors in which we are invited to look at ourselves, who are we in this parable? The Trappist monk, Father Thomas Keating, O.C.S.O., suggests that we are the unjust judge and the widow represents the Kingdom of God.

The widow is the Kingdom of God, i.e., grace that is constantly banging on our door—morning, noon, and night—pleading, "Do me justice," or more specifically, "How about spending some time in prayer? How about forgiving your enemy? How about seeking reconciliation with your brother-in-law? How about helping someone in need?"

Or again, "Accept the dark side of your personality. Take note of the feelings that hinder your relationships, your efforts to forgive and not to judge. Where are these feelings coming from? Why do you keep excluding those people from your life?" These are the things that the divine widow—the Kingdom of God—has in mind when she pleads, "Do me justice!" In other words, "Be compassionate as your heavenly Father is compassionate."

The divine widow keeps pounding on the door of our hearts day after day, as we try to put her off. That means the Kingdom of God keeps pounding on the door of our hearts day after day and we try to put off the Kingdom. If you think that modern forms of communication can be overwhelming, wait until you encounter how many ways of communicating God can come up with. God approaches us all day long, coming to meet us morning, noon and night through people, events, our thoughts, feelings, memories, reactions, our failings, and even our sins. God is more "annoying" and insistent than all the bings and swooshes and other noises that you hear on your phone every time you get an e-mail or a text or a voice message. In fact, God approaches us so much that all the bings and swooshes and other noises are like one non-stop sound!

We accept the Kingdom finally, not because we are just and even less so because we deserve it, but because at some point, like the unjust judge, we cannot stand God's grace nagging and persisting at us anymore. Like the unjust judge we just can't take it anymore and we give up. We are forced to give in saying, "Okay, God, take my life. I am in your hands."

This is the point of this parable. The mercy of God is constantly knocking on the door of our hearts, 24/7 as they say. Eventually we give in to God. God's mercy will eventually win out and take us over. It's just a matter of time. God won't stop until his mercy saves every one of us. We can't lose! God always wins.

Lord Jesus Christ, Son of the Living God,
have mercy on me, a sinner.

Being Mercy:
Beyond Merit, Way Beyond Merit

M ost of us are familiar with the parable known
as the "Parable of the Workers and the Vineyard." In brief, the parable tells us that at various in-
tervals during the day—6:00 a.m., 9:00 a.m., noon,
3:00 p.m., and 5:00 p.m.—the landowner went to
the marketplace and hired more people. He did not
negotiate. He simply told them, "I will pay you what
is right." We hear that even at the eleventh hour he
went out again and found a few idlers who had been
hanging around all day. They were probably already
half-drunk or had a hangover from the night before.
So they stumbled out into the vineyard, picked a few
grapes, and then it was time to quit.

People often think that this parable is about the
generosity of the landowner...Hardly. Ask the people
who went to work at 6:00 a.m. if they think that the

landowner was generous. In addition to paying those who worked for five minutes the same as they, they were paid a denarius, which would have been the minimum wage for peasants. This is not generosity.

The landowner's behavior seems unjust and unfair. Those listening to the parable would naturally have sided with the workers who felt they were mistreated, even though they received what they contracted for. Most of us would want to side with the workers who went out early to the vineyard at the crack of dawn.

I remember making a retreat at a Trappist monastery in California one July. One day we were invited to pick grapes with the monks, so I volunteered to do so. It's much more romantic as an idea than actually doing it! And I remember thinking that when I get to heaven I'm going to find those people who are in heaven but didn't start picking grapes until late in the day…and I plan to have a word or two with them!

This parable raises questions about the standard of justice in the Kingdom of God. Should not those who have worked more hours be given more? Evidently, entry into the Kingdom of God is not a question of merit.

Human standards of judgment are turned upside down in this parable. Ordinary standards of justice cannot explain how the kingdom works. Justification and holiness are gifts and they have nothing to do with social status or with personal merit. Words like "merit" should make us uncomfortable, because there is almost always a subtle form of pride in meriting something.

This parable can greatly upset those of us who were trained in pre-Vatican II Catholicism. We piled up our good works and our good deeds—going to Mass on Sundays, spending time in prayer, abstaining from meat on Fridays, giving alms during Lent, etc.—so that the punishment due to our sins would be cancelled out.

The Church no longer teaches this way, but the temptation remains for us to think this way. The Trappist monk, Father Thomas Keating, O.C.S.O., writes that we ought to thank God when our prayer is completely dry, when we get no special favors. If we get special favors from God, we might be in great trouble. We might slip into the presumption that our good deeds earned those gifts. They did not. We must trust in God's mercy and not in our own spiritual experiences or accomplishments.

So how do we get into the kingdom if it is not something that we can earn? We enter the Kingdom of God not by merit, but by consenting to God's gracious invitation.

In this parable grace is symbolized by the need of the landowner for more workers, and it seems to be urgent, since the landowner went out every couple or hours to find more workers.

Grace is God's need to respond to our need. God has to respond, so to speak, to our needs. In this parable, God's response is directed to the people standing in the marketplace, idle and wasting their time—gambling, drinking, gossiping, snoozing or whatever.

Their behavior does not merit anything, but their need is great. That's the point—it is their *need* that Jesus is responding to. Therefore his behavior subverts our general ideas of how to win God's favor. We do not win it. God's mercy is evoked in direct proportion to our misery—to our lack of inner and outer resources. Our need is what creates God's need to reach out to us and to pour out his mercy upon us.

The invitation to enter the kingdom goes forth again and again and again. No one is forced to accept. The invitation is extended because of the total generosity and goodness of God. The very definition of mercy is that it responds to need. God's greatest gift is to offer us the divine life itself. This is why Jesus reached out to public sinners. He had to show his Father's urgent concern for those most in need of his grace and help.

Grace and help, of course, are just as free for the well-behaved. It's just that they often do not realize this.

The bottom line of this parable is that the kingdom is not based on human standards of justice and equity, but on the infinite mercy of God, whose principal need is to respond to the desperate state of the human condition, the state that we all share in!

The fallen and human condition is where the kingdom is most active. Jesus came in the flesh to express the infinite concern of the Father for our sins. The spiritual journey enables us more and more to appreciate the divine goodness. Acceptance of the invitation is the key to belonging to the kingdom.

We recognize that God is boundless and infinite compassion. It is because God is our Father and Mother that we are invited to the kingdom. Reason will not get us there. Good deeds will not get us there. The kingdom is sheer gift, sheer gift.

A possible problem of a faithful and virtuous life is that it can create the sense of having earned something from God and thus misses the point that it is an invitation. Justification does not come through good works but through the divine greatness. Good deeds are essential, but only insofar as they are a sign of gratitude to God for all that God has done for us.

When I was a boy I was kind to my father because I feared him. I didn't want to get into trouble with him. I didn't want to get spanked or punished. Now, at age 61, I am kind to my father because he has been kind and generous and loving and good to me all my life. I can make no other response but to be kind to him. I am no longer afraid of being punished by him. Rather I only want to show my gratitude to him. Thus, in the Christian life, intention and motivation are very important.

Spiritual progress is the sheer gift of God. God

is not waiting to crown us with a halo for our good deeds. God is waiting to forgive us for our sins and press us to his heart as little children in desperate need of boundless love.

This parable announces that human standards of judgment have no place in the kingdom. A new standard is present, which is God's infinite need to show us mercy.

Perhaps you've had the experience of eating dinner at a restaurant and, when you go to pay the bill, the cashier says, "It's already been taken care of." Someone else who saw you there paid for you.

That's how it is with Our Lord. He's already paid. There's no admission fee—already paid. Already taken care of. Nothing to pay for. Nothing to merit. Nothing to earn. Only to be grateful.

Lord Jesus Christ, Son of the Living God,
have mercy on me, a sinner.

Being Mercy:
Accepting Mercy from an Enemy

The Parable of the Good Samaritan is well known to believers and non-believers. There are hospitals named Good Samaritan. Most states have Good Samaritan laws that offer legal protection to people who voluntarily help an injured person.

To understand the full meaning of this story we need to understand two important things. First, this story is a parable. And a parable is a story told by Jesus, the intent of which is to question your values; to question what you think; to turn your world upside down, so to speak; to encourage you to ask why you think what you think.

And second, to better understand what Jesus wanted to teach in this parable we need to be aware of the Jewish hierarchical society of the time. The priest, the Levite, and the Israelite lay person were the familiar triad of that society. In addition to the triad, those who belonged to Israel—insiders—were sharply distinguished from those who did not belong—outsiders.

Samaritans were looked upon not only as outsiders, but as the mortal enemies of Israel and defectors from the Jewish religion. For those listening to Jesus' parable, a Samaritan was totally unacceptable.

The reason that the priest and the Levite pass by the victim is not addressed. The law commanded that priests and Levites were not to bury the dead. But the Gospel tells us that the man was "half dead." The priest and the Levite had no excuse to pass him by without helping.

The build-up of suspense then focuses on who the next person coming down the road will be. The listeners had to be thinking that it would be an Israelite lay person. He will appear in the role of the hero and bind up the wounds of the injured man. Then they can all go home reinforced in their usual way of thinking, in their black-and-white world, in their world of who is in and who is out—which, sad to say, is what we often want anyway—to not change the way we think about certain people or ethnic groups or whatever.

Jesus, being the master storyteller that he is, actually tells the story in such a way so as to encourage the expectation that the next person to come down the road will be an Israelite lay person, on the lowest rung on the social ladder, but still one of their own and therefore acceptable.

But who comes down the road instead? It was a Samaritan, the mortal enemy of the Jewish nation and of the Jewish religion. After their shock that it was a Samaritan, the listeners' first thought probably was, "He'll just finish off the poor guy and kill him."

But the Samaritan, as you know, ministers to the wounded man. He takes the injured man to an inn and pays for his stay. The story ends with the hearers scratching their heads, leaving them without anybody in the story with whom to identify. They cannot identify with the priest or the Levite because they were merciless. They cannot identify with the victim. And it is inconceivable for most of them to identify with the Samaritan. That would be to accept the compassion and mercy of their mortal enemy.

As I said earlier, parables have as their point to subvert the way of thinking of those who are listening, to turn their world upside down. So the message that is being communicated in this parable is that the Kingdom of God knows no political or religious or ethnic or cultural boundaries. The old maps of Israelite society are not relevant in the new kingdom. In the kingdom that Jesus is preaching, there are no rigid barriers between insiders and outsiders.

The implications of Jesus' teachings are especially important today for two reasons: (1) humanity is moving more and more toward a global society with interaction among peoples in every conceivable way: economic, social, political, and religious; and (2) so many people and countries want to build walls and keep everyone out rather than welcome and invite others in.

The Trappist monk, Father Thomas Keating, O.C.S.O., asks if the first hearers of Jesus would have understood the Kingdom of God as Jesus preached it unless the one who came down the road was a Samaritan instead of the expected Israelite? Probably not. And we have to ask ourselves…will we ever overcome our various forms of prejudice unless we are confronted by opposition or tragedy or the "enemy"? The Kingdom of God may be most active in what is most unacceptable to us, whoever or whatever that might be.

If only we could believe this—that the Kingdom of God might be most active in what is most unacceptable

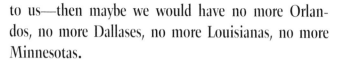

to us—then maybe we would have no more Orlandos, no more Dallases, no more Louisianas, no more Minnesotas.

Let me tell you a modern-day parable. A man is putting up signs in his front yard that read: "English only." "Deport the illegals." "Go back to where you came from." And while putting the signs in the ground, he has a heart attack and falls over. At the same time two undocumented men, who do not speak English, are walking by and see what just happened. They give him CPR and save his life. This man would have been forced to accept the kindness and mercy of people he could not stand. The Kingdom of God may be most active in us when we are forced to accept the kindness and mercy of people we cannot stand.

So this parable is not really a story about a nice guy who helps an injured man. It's about *who* the nice guy is and *why* Jesus would choose him to be part of the story. The parable of the Good Samaritan challenges our values. We are forced to acknowledge the mercy of those we distrust or those we can't stand and situations that we find most unacceptable.

The parables of Jesus always leave the listener with

unresolved questions. The parable of the Good Samaritan asks the question, "What is your idea of the Kingdom of God?"

To enter the Kingdom of God is to move beyond social expectations. Jesus identifies the action of the Kingdom of God with the compassion and mercy of the Samaritan. Our supposed enemy may turn out to be our greatest benefactor. This is true of people and of situations and of what lies inside of us. Our supposed enemy—those people or that situation or this part of me—may turn out to be our greatest benefactor.

The Kingdom of God has no fixed social, ethnic, racial, nationalistic, economic, or religious boundaries. There are no insiders or outsiders, no elite or non-elite. The Father whom Jesus reveals is the God of the human race as one family. Everyone must be concerned about everyone else. Unconditional love and relentless mercy are the names of God.

Lord Jesus Christ, Son of the Living God,
have mercy on me, a sinner.

Being Mercy:
A Mission of Mercy
to the Pacific Northwest

S ome months ago I received an invitation from Archbishop Peter Sartain, Archbishop of Seattle to come to the Archdiocese of Seattle to preach on the Year of Mercy, to hear confessions, and to celebrate Masses. I gladly accepted his invitation.

I arrived on Friday, September 30. That evening I preached at a Holy Hour for Mercy at Holy Family Parish in south Seattle. It's in a part of the city known as White Center. For as long as people can remember, it has been the place where immigrants have lived after arriving. The community today is filled with recent immigrants from Mexico. I was told that prior to Mexicans, there were Cambodians. And prior to Cambodians, there were Laotians.

I heard confessions from 5:30 until 7:00 p.m. I heard one confession in English and dozens in

Spanish. I felt like I was back at St. John Vianney Parish in Goodyear, Arizona, where I served as pastor for 12 years—from 1990 to 2002. I heard those "same" confessions for many years as immigrants try to make sense of life in another country, try to practice their faith in another setting, try to understand their children who live between cultures.

On Saturday morning there was a "Rosary for Vocations" at the Cathedral Parish in Seattle. The Cathedral is Seattle is really beautiful. I heard confessions from 9:30 a.m. until the Rosary started at 11:00 a.m. The first person came into the reconciliation room, sat down, and said, "Bless me Father, for I have sinned. My last confession was 62 years ago. These are my sins." It's a good thing that I was sitting down or I might have fallen down. Sixty-two years is longer than I have been alive! The person said, "I wanted to be the first one so I wouldn't change my mind while waiting in line."

The tenderness and humanity and warmth of Pope Francis have invited thousands of people to come back to practicing their faith. He has made a whole Church feel at home in our humanity. He has helped us all realize our common need for mercy. Cathedrals always draw all sorts of people—from professional people to street people and everyone in between, people without high school diplomas and people with doctorates, people who live in the suburbs and people who live in the shadow of the Cathedral, and so many more.

On Saturday evening I was at St. Pius X Parish in Mountlake Terrace, Washington—a typical parish, if there is such a thing. Three weekend Masses in English, one in Spanish. After the 5:30 p.m. Saturday Vigil Mass I gave a talk and then heard lots of confessions until 9:00 p.m.—good people trying to love God.

On Sunday morning I was not prepared for the grace that God would give me. I drove to Prince of Peace Mission in Belfair. It's over 70 miles from Seattle around the Puget Sound. I could have taken the Bremerton Ferry across the water but I decided to drive. It was a beautiful drive.

As I walked into the church an elderly couple came up to me and said: "You probably don't remember us, but we are Brian's parents…" Then I remembered. Brian was a student at the University of Portland when I was assigned there in the 1980s. I hired him to be one of my RAs when I was Rector of Villa Maria Hall. Sometime around 2006 or so his wife died in a tragic accident and Brian asked me to do the funeral. It was so nice to see his parents again, to ask about Brian, to ask about Brian's children.

The schedule that was prepared for me by the Archdiocese read "Mass in Spanish, bilingual confessions, and bilingual talk after Mass." As soon as I walked into the church I noticed that everyone was Guatemalan, not the Mexican community that I imagined would be there. I heard confessions from 11:00 a.m. until 1:00 p.m. The people had been told that I am bilingual. And I am. But somehow many of the people thought being bilingual meant that I spoke Spanish and Q'anjob'al, one of the 23 indigenous dialects of Guatemala. Lots of people came to confession. Most of the women spoke Q'anjob'al. Most of the men spoke Spanish and Q'anjob'al. And the school-age children spoke Spanish and Q'anjob'al and English.

I heard many confessions in Q'anjob'al. I just sat there and listened. I cried. I didn't need to understand a single word as people sat or kneeled in front of me and confessed their sins. I could simply feel their sorrow, their contrition, their desire to receive the mercy and forgiveness of God—such beautiful and lovely and wonderful and humble people. I felt completely unworthy to be in their presence, let alone hearing their confessions. I cried some more. The need for mercy and forgiveness is universal.

The other thing I kept thinking was how much I love the Church. There I was, a priest hearing confessions in a language I could not understand. It truly is Christ who welcomes, Christ who forgives, Christ who offers his mercy—all through me, unprofitable and sinful instrument that I am. Christ does all this without my needing to know what is going on. The Holy Father reminded us Missionaries of Mercy of this several times in his talk to us last February: It is *Christ* who is present in the sacrament.

After confessions I celebrated Mass and the people did not need to be told to participate with full voice and heart. They don't know how not to! The Mass was so beautiful—and all the women were dressed in really beautiful Guatemalan dresses. Then following the Mass there was the veneration of the relics of St. Faustina, the saint who made famous the devotion to

Divine Mercy. Following the confessions, the Mass and the veneration of the relics, there was a wonderful lunch with Guatemalan tamales—to die for...totally delicious!

After lunch I drove to Portland. On Monday morning I gave a talk on the Year of Mercy to about 120 girls at St. Mary's Academy, a Catholic high school for girls in Portland.

Such different experiences over the past four days—different settings, different languages, different experiences of life, and different ways of approaching God—and yet one common theme: our need for mercy. Is it any wonder that the Year of Mercy continues to "grow" throughout the world and the Church? I believe more than ever what I've been saying since the Year of Mercy began: The Holy Spirit gave Pope Francis an extraordinary grace to read the signs of the times...and then to proclaim a Year of Mercy. This Year has been a rich gift and blessing and source of so much grace to the world and to the Church.

Lord Jesus Christ, Son of the Living God,
have mercy on me, a sinner.

Being Mercy:
An Unforgettable Stop along the Way

S erving the Church as a Missionary of Mercy during this Extraordinary Jubilee Year of Mercy has been, as Thomas Merton wrote, "mercy within mercy within mercy." A best part of the year has been this. Every time I am asked to talk on the "Mercy of God," I believe in it—and experience it—that much more. I am so grateful.

While this year has been filled with memorable moments of grace and mercies without end, there was one unexpected grace and mercy along the way. Earlier this fall I had the chance to visit a first cousin whom I had not seen in more than 30 years. She was born the year that I came to Notre Dame as a first-year student, so I never really knew her. I would see her when I went home for Christmas and for the summer, and while I was in formation for the priesthood I saw her off and on. Though I am not entirely certain, I think that the last time I saw her was when I was ordained a priest in 1984; she was 12.

For many years she worked in the "adult industry" and was widely known all around the country and even beyond. I would hear of her off and on over the years. I thought of her many, many times over those years and prayed for her safety in what is a rough and dark world that most of us cannot even imagine.

About 16 months ago she left the adult industry and wrote her autobiography. My sister told me about the book and I ordered a copy directly from the author because I was hoping that she would see my name. Less than a week after I placed my order, I received the book in the mail and found that, on the inside front cover, she had written, "Dear Cousin Joe...." When I read those three words I started to cry. In her note, she offered her e-mail address and invited me to send her an e-mail, which I promptly did.

We corresponded off and on via e-mail and text for several months, and then I asked if I could stop by and visit her the next time I would be in her neck of the woods. She readily accepted. And so earlier this fall I stopped by her home for what turned out to be a four-hour visit of grace and mercy for both of us.

I did not know what expectations to have for our visit. I hoped and prayed that we would be able to talk and visit. I did not see myself as going to save her. Jesus has already done that—and much better than I ever could! I also did not see myself as going to talk with her about God's mercy and love. Rather I went with the hope of engaging in what the Holy Father calls "the culture of encounter." The other has something good to give to me and I have something good to give to the other.

After twenty minutes of small talk, we spoke of our lives, of memories of our grandmother (who was so important in both of our lives), of our cousins (we have many of them!), of moments of clarity and moments of darkness along the way, of periods of hope and periods of despair, of dreams fulfilled and dreams unfulfilled, of the promptings and movements of God in our lives over the past thirty years, and of so much more.

She told me that she had started to go to Mass again. It was so clear to me that this widely known star in the adult industry was above all else a child of God—not an object, not a thing, not a commodity, but a person—a person with a life history, with feelings, with hopes and dreams, with a mind and a heart and soul, made in the image and likeness of God, cherished and loved by God forever.

We talked. We cried. We shared. We told stories. We cried some more. We asked questions. We wondered. We listened to one another. We were a vessel of God's mercy and love for one another. We could have talked for four more hours. I didn't want our visit to end.

I would guess that the most confessed sin that I hear in the confessional is that of looking at pornography. After visiting with my cousin I think that a good penance might be this: pray for the people that one is viewing. This would help the penitent to know firsthand that the person they are viewing is, above all, a person.

I am so grateful to God for the opportunity of having visited with my cousin. She taught me so much about the relentless mercy of God. I can only hope that my visit was also helpful to her in accepting the mercy of God. Since we are all sinners, we all stand in need of the mercy of God. No one is "too bad" to not receive it. No one is "too good" to not need it. God's mercy is saving us at every moment of our existence. It will save us until the end and it will see us into the next life.

> Lord Jesus Christ, Son of the Living God,
> have mercy on me, a sinner.

Being Mercy:
The Day I Got to
Embrace the Holy Father...

*S*unday, November 20, Feast of Jesus Christ, King of the Universe and the Closing Mass of the Jubilee Year of Mercy...

I arrived at St. Peter's Square at 8:00 a.m. for the 10:00 a.m. Mass. There had to be already 20,000 people in line trying to get through security. After running into several dead ends, thanks to an Italian priest, I found my way to the entrance for priest concelebrants.

I went through security and found my way to the concelebrant section, which was on the "ground" level of the piazza towards the front. The altar was on the "top" level of the piazza. On either side of the altar there were chairs for several hundred people. On the one side of the altar there would be lay people and

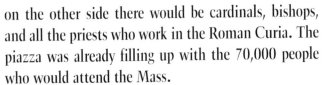

on the other side there would be cardinals, bishops, and all the priests who work in the Roman Curia. The piazza was already filling up with the 70,000 people who would attend the Mass.

When I arrived at the section of priest concelebrants I was asked if I would help distribute communion. Of course, I would. To my left were tables filled with bowls of hosts and chalices with wine—an amazing sight to behold. Exactly at 10:00 a.m. the Mass began with the closing of the Holy Door. I could not see the Pope from where I was sitting but I could see him on a big-screen TV. I have so loved this Holy Year of Mercy that I thought about sneaking into St. Peter's and getting behind the door so that when the Holy Father tried to close the door it wouldn't close! Watching the Holy Father close the Door of Mercy and listening to the prayer he prayed was beautiful.

Then the Mass began. At the Creed, each of us in the concelebrant section were handed a bowl of hosts and a chalice of wine. Well, there went any chance of scratching my nose from then until after communion! At the time of the Consecration, all the concelebrants lifted up the bowls and the chalices. After the Lamb of

God we were all directed to stations. I realized that I would be bringing communion to priest concelebrants who were not distributing communion. So I went to each priest with the Body and Blood of Christ. The priest would take a host and then dip the host into the Precious Blood and then receive it.

When I was finished I asked the M.C. how I was supposed to receive communion. He said, *"in Basilica dopo"* ("in the Basilica afterwards"). So when I finished bringing communion to my section of priests, I followed the other priests and walked into the Basilica all the way around the piazza, into the Apostolic Palace, and into the Basilica, thereby getting in my 10,000 steps for the day!

It was amazing to see the Basilica on the inside with no one in there except for priests who were returning the Body and Blood of Christ. The Basilica is huge. I put the Body and Blood of Christ on the table, received communion, and followed all the other priests out of the Basilica back into the piazza. When I went out the doors I was on the "top" level. The Pope was about 25 yards from me. And I said to myself, "I'm not going back to my seat. I'm staying up here." So I

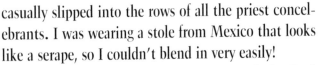

casually slipped into the rows of all the priest concelebrants. I was wearing a stole from Mexico that looks like a serape, so I couldn't blend in very easily!

Then there was the closing prayer and the final blessing. And little by little I began to inch my way to the front row of the priests and then I finally made it to the front row. There was a dividing line between the priests and the bishops and cardinals, and about 10 secret service men in the row dividing the priests from the bishops. I said to one of them (in Italian), "I forgot my red hat." He looked at me and said, "*Non e vero, Padre.*" ("That's not true, Father.") Okay, it wasn't true. But when you're that near the Pope, you'll try anything to get closer!

After the final blessing there was a very brief ceremony. Pope Francis had written an Apostolic Letter—Mercy and Misery—to commemorate the end of the Year of Mercy. He had hand-signed six copies of it and six delegations of people came forward from all parts of the world to receive the letter. When this finished, all the bishops and priests began to leave the altar area.

The Pope walked toward the cardinals, and I saw

that the Pope was going to greet every cardinal one by one. There were about 50 of them. I was about 15 yards from him at this point. While he was doing this, a long line of priests had formed, all hoping that the Holy Father would greet the priests present. I don't remember exactly how it happened, but I was part of this row. During this entire time I became fast friends with Alessandro, one of the secret service guys who told me "*Aspetti, Padre*" ("Wait, Father") each time I lunged forward. Sure enough when the Holy Father greeted the last cardinal, he went over to the priests and began to greet them one by one. He would smile, shake hands, and move to the next priest.

I thought of how tired he must be. It was already noon. Mass had begun at 10:00 a.m., and yet I could see him smiling at each person whose hand he shook. It made me think back to when I was a pastor and would greet people after Mass. I know that I didn't smile at every person, especially when I was tired. Yet the Pope kept smiling and shaking hands and he had to be tired.

As he got closer and closer to me I thought that this is really going to happen. I am going to shake hands and speak with the Pope, the Holy Father, the Supreme Pontiff, the Vicar of Christ on earth. He came and stood right in front of me. I didn't even think about what to do...or if I should do it. I did what was natural when you love someone. I embraced him and I kissed him.

Then I spoke to him in Spanish, "Thank you so much, Holy Father, for sending me as a Missionary of Mercy." He said, "You are still one. This ministry is to be ongoing." I told him that I would be honored to keep serving the Church as a Missionary of Mercy. Then I thanked him for all that he has done for the Church and for the People of God. And I told him that I love him. I took out my rosary from my pocket and asked him to bless it. He did. I learned the next day by reading his Apostolic Letter—Mercy and Misery—that he has asked the Missionaries of Mercy to continue in this role for the indefinite future.

When the Pope spoke to me he was entirely present to me. It was as though there was no one else there but me. I wanted to remain in his presence, to hold on to him, to look at him, to hug him again, and to tell him how much I have learned from him and how

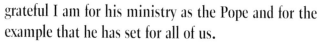

grateful I am for his ministry as the Pope and for the example that he has set for all of us.

Why did I want to meet him so desperately? Well, part of it is, of course, that he is the Pope; but it's much more than that. It's because of who he is as a person, as a disciple of Jesus, as a fellow sinner whose sins are forgiven. He is an amazing man who has invited the entire world to accept the mercy of God and to extend it to everyone around us.

I still can't believe that I hugged the Pope! I will never forget that moment of grace. Thank you, Pope Francis. Thank you, Jesus.

And never go back to your seat!

Lord Jesus Christ, Son of the Living God,
have mercy on me, a sinner.

Being Mercy:
One Year Ago Today

O ne year ago today—December 22, 2015—I was working on the possibility of an ACE project in Monterrey, Nuevo Leon, Mexico. I woke up in a hotel room to an e-mail informing me that my name had been submitted to Pope Francis to serve as a Missionary of Mercy for the Jubilee Year of Mercy. And the e-mail read, "...the Holy Father has gladly accepted your name...."

I can still feel the emotion from that moment—I was excited and humbled. I remember thinking that I have received a lifetime of mercy from God; and, with all the zeal of a young man, I wanted to extend that mercy, to preach about that mercy, to offer that mercy to whomever I could. What I did not know at the time is the effect that serving as a Missionary of Mercy would have on me.

Serving as a Missionary of Mercy has been an incredible gift and grace from God. During this year I have been asked to give talks on mercy more times than I can count. I never got tired of giving these talks—to priests, to presbyterates, to parish groups, to high school students, to students at Notre Dame, to seminars, and so much more. And each time I would give a talk, as I spoke, God convinced me even more of his relentless mercy, of his forgiveness, of his desire to show us mercy and tenderness and love. I would often think, "I hope that someone besides me is getting something out of this talk because I am more convinced of this than the last time I gave a talk on mercy."

When the Holy Father commissioned us to serve as Missionaries of Mercy on Ash Wednesday in 2016, he asked us to make ourselves available to hear confessions as often as we could—and so I tried to do this. I do not know how many confessions I heard during this year—hundreds, perhaps more than a thousand. It does not matter. God has given me the opportunity to extend his mercy and forgiveness to countless people. I will always be grateful for this gift.

"Bless me, Father, for I have sinned. It has been

62 years since my last confession…"; "Bless me, Father, for I have sinned. I am so ashamed and embarrassed by what I am about to tell you…"; "Bless me, Father, for I have sinned. I am not sure where to begin…"; "Bless me, Father, for I have sinned. I am caught in a cycle of sin.…"

Each confession is an opportunity for grace to flow back and forth, for certainly God's grace is always a two-way street. As a confessor I have been so moved and touched and edified and humbled by people's confessions, by people's struggles to live a good life. The confessor is always enriched and changed by people's confessions. Every time a priest hears a confession, he himself receives grace and mercy.

The Holy Father reminded us of several things when he spoke to us last February. Three thoughts have guided me when I have had the privilege of hearing confessions: (1) "Smile when people come to confession"; (2) "When you enter the confessional, remember that you enter as a sinner and that you are the first in need of mercy and forgiveness"; (3) "Always remember that it is Christ who receives the penitent. It is Christ who listens. It is Christ who absolves sins." Such great advice! (1) It's easy for me to smile; (2) My sin is always before me. I have no problem remembering that I am a sinner; (3) The confessions that I heard in Q'anjob'al (a language that I do not understand or speak) powerfully reminded me that it is Christ who does everything in this sacrament. Remembering these points makes hearing confessions a joy, a happiness, a great grace, a cause for giving thanks to God.

During this Year of Mercy I have had the opportunity to meet Pope Francis twice. The first time I was only able to touch his hand, to kiss his hand, and to tell him that I love him. The second time I was able to embrace him, to hug him, to speak with him, and to tell him again that I love him. People will often ask me if these opportunities were the highlights of this "Year of Mercy" for me. These moments with the Holy Father are moments that I will never forget. They are in me forever. But they are not the highlights of the Year of Mercy.

The highlights of the Year of Mercy are these. There have been times during this year when God has used me to help others accept his mercy and forgiveness for something that they had not accepted God's mercy and forgiveness previously. God has worked through this sinner to help someone else be open to God's relentless mercy and tender forgiveness and unconditional love. When this has happened, I am so grateful to God. Without a doubt, these are the highlights of the Year of Mercy.

Like so many other people I was so sad to see the Year of Mercy come to an end, but only the "official" year comes to an end. The mercy of God is, of course, without end, without limit. As the Holy Father noted in his Apostolic Letter "Mercy and Misery" promulgated on the last day of the Year of Mercy, "Mercy is not a parenthesis in the life of the Church. Rather it is the very foundation of the Church." As we pray in Psalm 136, "for his mercy endures forever...for his mercy endures forever."

I was, of course, delighted to learn from the Holy Father that he has asked the Missionaries of Mercy to continue in this role indefinitely. In his Apostolic Letter he wrote:

> I thank every Missionary of Mercy for this valuable service aimed at rendering effective

the grace of forgiveness. This extraordinary ministry does not end with the closing of the Holy Door. I wish it to continue until further notice as a concrete sign that the grace of the Jubilee remains alive and effective the world over. As a direct expression of my concern and closeness to the Missionaries of Mercy in this period, the Pontifical Council for Promoting the New Evangelization will supervise them and find the most suitable forms for the exercise of this valuable ministry.

I received an e-mail a few days ago from the Pontifical Council for the Promotion of the New Evangelization, the Council charged with overseeing the Year of Mercy and the Missionaries of Mercy. The e-mail informed me that details of what continuing to serve as a Missionary of Mercy will mean are forthcoming. In the meanwhile, I am very grateful for the opportunity to continue extending the mercy of God and for continuing to be a grateful recipient of this mercy. I need it today and I will need it forever. Thanks be to God, for his mercy endures forever....

Lord Jesus Christ, Son of the Living God, have mercy on me, a sinner.

Being Mercy:
Praying with Everyone

About a month before Christmas break, I decided that I would make a mini-retreat of four days at a Trappistine Abbey where I have made retreats many times over the past years. It is a place that I especially love. And I love the community of Sisters at the abbey. Like most Trappist and Trappistine monasteries and abbeys, it's very rural and in the middle of nowhere. Actually you can get to nowhere faster and easier than you can get to this wonderful and beautiful and life-giving abbey.

I would be there over the weekend of December 31 / January 1. There is a parish about 16 miles from the abbey and a mission of the parish about five miles from the abbey. I recalled my 19 years as pastor and how tired the pastor is after Advent and Christmas, so I decided to call the pastor of the parish and ask if he wanted any help over the weekend. In a brief conversation he asked me if I would take all the Masses—two at the parish church and one at the mission. I agreed to do so.

Both the parish and the mission have very small, tight-knit communities—everyone knows everyone. As soon as I walked in, everyone knew that I was a visitor. They were warm and welcoming—and wondering who this guy was! (I was not wearing black clerical clothing when I arrived.)

Both communities are very rural. There were a total of about 150 people who attended all three Masses. One thing that you notice after a few moments is that these communities have been kept together by the laity over many years. Pastors and Administrators have come and gone; and I wouldn't be surprised if, at times, there was no pastor. At the parish church, the person performing the music played the guitar and has been in charge of the music there since the Second Vatican Council! She's 95. Can you imagine? And she's still going strong and leading the singing.

While celebrating the second of the three Masses, during the first reading, as I looked out at the people, it became very clear to me that I did not favor the candidate that they most likely voted for in the recent election. And that got me thinking.

I'm sorry to admit that I didn't pay much attention to the readings or the responsorial psalm that day. I just kept pondering these thoughts: We voted for different candidates. I'm sure that these are good people. They are doing their best, trying to love God and their neighbor—so am I. How could I dislike them? How could I think ill of them? They are trying—so am I. They are failing and succeeding—so am I. They want a better future for their children—so do I. The more I looked at them, the more impossible it was for me to vilify them or to think of them as the enemy, as people I dislike, as people I can't stand.

January 20 is right around the corner and a new president will be installed, and we will have to support him as much as we are able. What common ground can I find with these people? I have always known that there are good Catholics on both sides of every issue. And, as much as I wanted to dislike them, I just couldn't. I kept thinking, "For God's sake, we're at the Eucharist together and here I am trying to find ways to dislike these people." But thankfully I could not. God is good!

We have just finished an Extraordinary Jubilee Year of Mercy. During this year the Holy Father has constantly encouraged us to expand our sense of mercy. It's not just being nice or kind. Rather, it is engaging in the culture of encounter, which Pope Francis defines quite simply: "I have something good to give to you. And you have something good to give to me." Just looking at the people that God had put in front of me that weekend made me know that it is true. They have something good to give to me, and I have something good to give to them.

After Mass we did not talk politics at the coffee and donuts. We simply visited and talked and shared hopes for the New Year—the hope that God would be revealed to us moment by moment, day by day, week by week, month by month.

Like all other years, 2017 will be a year of grace. By "a year of grace," I mean this: Everything is a grace. What a difference it would make if I were to welcome everything that happens to me as good news. It may require some extra digging in some situations to get beneath the surface to discover the grace of God. How much agony I would save myself if I really believed, as St. Paul writes in his Letter to the Romans, that nothing can separate us from the love of God. If I truly believe that nothing can separate me from the love of God, then I can live life with a confidence that allows me to greet every new situation with a childlike hope that is the exact opposite of the dread and anguish that so many people feel in facing the future.

On January 1 we celebrated the Feast of Mary, Mother of God. You can be sure that when Mary, at age 14, stood in front of a new year (however the calendar was when she lived), she did not think that one day, while she was having a cup of hot chocolate with marshmallows, the Angel Gabriel would visit her and ask her to become the Mother of God.

But because she had learned to trust in God completely, she said "yes" to a mystery that she did not understand and, in fact, never quite understood fully.

So hope exists that in some hidden way God is working through every situation to bring about good. It is with this faith and expectancy that God invites us to welcome 2017.

With this faith, then, it doesn't really matter if what we are experiencing is joy or pain, because both joy and pain are graces of God. As St. Thérèse of Lisieux writes, "Everything is a grace." Everything.

What Christ promises and has won for us by his death and resurrection is grace upon grace upon grace, mercy within mercy within mercy. When we say "HAPPY NEW YEAR" to one another, the deepest meaning of what we are saying is this: May you find God's grace and mercy in 2017 at every moment, in every person, in every situation, in every event, at every turn, and always within yourself.

What a moment of grace and mercy it was for me to celebrate the Eucharist with people I would not have chosen. Mercy makes it possible for us to pray with everyone!

Lord Jesus Christ, Son of the Living God,
have mercy on me, a sinner.

Being Mercy:
Notre Dame Story Nights

"My Notre Dame Story began when I was born. I think that my parents took me home from the hospital in a Notre Dame onesie!"

"My Notre Dame Story began when I was six. My mom and my little brother and I lay down in a big wooden crate that was tacked under a tractor trailer in Tijuana, and that's how we crossed the border from Mexico to get into the United States."

"I'm the kid that, on football Saturdays, when I was three years old I was already dressed up as a Notre Dame cheerleader."

"Both my parents went to Harvard. Two of my uncles went to Harvard. My heart was all set on going to Harvard and playing lacrosse there. When I didn't get in, I was crushed. I came to Notre Dame, certainly not my first choice. And now I am so happy and so grateful to be here."

Diversity is certainly becoming a way of life. You can't go anywhere and not hear people talking about diversity and inclusion. It's wonderful. Though I am only 50% Italian, I grew up in a very Italian world. We belonged to an Italian national parish and I went to the parish grade school. I always say that I didn't know anyone whose last name did not end in a vowel until I went to high school. In my parish, diversity meant whether you were from Castel di Lucio or Palermo or Aquadolce or Santo Stefano di Camastra!

When I went to Notre Dame as an undergraduate (1972-1976) Notre Dame was not very diverse. When I returned here in 2009 to work in ACE and to live in a dorm, I was surprised and gladdened at how much more diverse Notre Dame had become. Notre Dame has been very intentional about creating a more diverse student body than I had known as an undergraduate student.

At the same time I was concerned because I noticed that students did not mix easily or readily across racial, cultural, ethnic, or economic backgrounds. It is not uncommon to go to South Dining Hall and see a table filled with Latino students eating dinner together and talking in Spanish. Or you might go to La Fortune and see several tables of Asian students eating and studying together. I quickly realized that, for the most part, students do not meet other students across cultures because they simply do not know how to do it and do not have opportunities to do it. In addition, as human beings we seem hard wired to associate with those who look like we do, think like we do, and talk like we do.

Several years ago I decided that I would invite ten students to my room in Dillon one random evening. I blind copied all of them so that no one knew who else was coming. I told them that I would be serving pizza, and that everyone would have an opportunity to tell their "Notre Dame Story"—that is, each person would tell the story of how they came to Notre Dame.

Now four or five years later (I can't remember when I began) I have hosted about 80 of these gatherings which have come to be known as "Notre Dame Story Nights." More than 800 students have attended a Notre Dame Story Night. For the past three years I have invited only first-year students.

They have several more years at Notre Dame to build bridges across culture and to continue relationships that they began as first-year students.

I tell them the only purpose of the evening is that they meet other students from different cultures and races and ethnicities and economic backgrounds. I tell the students at the beginning of each gathering, "Some years ago two students who might not have ever met became roommates in one of Notre Dame's study-abroad programs. I'm going to keep hosting Notre Dame Story Nights until I get a wedding out of it." They all laugh…and look around the room.

The stories are beautiful and moving and personal and touching. "My great-grandfather went to school here—and then my grandfather and my father—and now me!" "I never heard of Notre Dame until my guidance counselor in high school mentioned it to me." "I was in a high school program called Avid. It's for high-performing, economically poor students. And through a program called Questbridge I learned about Notre Dame." "My high school English teacher was an ACE teacher. I learned all about Notre Dame from him." "All my siblings have gone

to Notre Dame and I was determined to go somewhere different. And here I am, happy as could be."
"I was sitting in my AP algebra class and I got an email telling me that I had been accepted." "I was waiting desperately for news from Notre Dame. For several days my mom and I would wait at the mailbox for the mail carrier to bring the mail. Then the day came—the BIG envelope—I opened it. I had been accepted. I started to cry. My mom was crying and so was the mail carrier! We all hugged each other and cried some more."

As I listen to each student's story, I am aware that every person's story is holy, is of God, and that we are all standing on holy ground. It's easy to see how God moves and acts and prompts in our lives. And the older I get, the more I know that all anyone really wants in life is for someone else to know a piece of their story.

Notre Dame Story Nights are an opportunity for our wonderful young people to share a piece of their story with other students who represent the growing diversity of Notre Dame. There are athletes, DACA students, international students, students from wealthy families, the guy down the hall, shy students, gregarious students, first-generation students, students working on campus in order to send money to their family in Texas, and so much more.

After everyone tells their Notre Dame Story, we all say our names again and then we pray the "Hail Mary" together. One night a student asked, "Can we all pray the Hail Mary in our native language?" We prayed the "Hail Mary" together that evening in Spanish, English, Lithuanian, and Swahili. It was so beautiful.

On the first Saturday of May, I invite all the students who have taken part in a Notre Dame Story Night for Mass and lunch. Of the 170 who will have participated, approximately 120 will come. It's a wonderful event each year.

These Notre Dame Story Nights are an opportunity to put into practice what Pope Francis consistently calls the "culture of encounter." You have something good to give to me, and I have something good to give to you. I think that all the students leave my room having experienced the culture of encounter that evening. Each one has received something good from the others. And each one has given something good to the others. As I clean up and haul out the trash, I think about how might our country and our world be enriched if people sat down with one another from different backgrounds and told part of their story. We would have a very different world. Rather than building walls, we would all be building bridges.

As I sit and listen I feel that the mercy of God is flowing in and out of everyone in the room. These wonderful young students truly listen to each other as they tell their Notre Dame Story. As I say so often, one thing is very obvious—we all stand in need of the mercy of God. For sure, the mercy of God unites all of us in our diversity. The mercy of God is all inclusive.

*Lord Jesus Christ, Son of the Living God,
have mercy on me, a sinner.*

Being Mercy:
Mercy and the LGBT Community

She sat in my office across from me and said to me, "I am 100% Catholic and I am 100% Lesbian. I am both these things to the core. I cannot imagine not being both." Her words touched my heart and soul.

He sat very comfortably, looked at me, and said, "I'm somewhere on the scale between gay and bi. I have known this since I was in grade school. I am also Catholic. I am proud to be a Catholic. I will always be Catholic. Even if the Church tells me that who I am sexually is somehow wrong, I know that before God, I am not. I want to be both. And I will be both." His words pierced my heart and soul.

The LGBT community at Notre Dame, like in so many places, is a shadow community. It has to hide itself. It doesn't reveal itself. It is known mainly to others in the same community. By and large, it cannot express itself as it might want to. It has been forced to go into hiding. It would like to live in the light—but that's easier said than done.

I believe that the LGBT population at Notre Dame might be as large as, or larger than, many of the other minority communities at Notre Dame. The LGBT population certainly cuts across culture, ethnicity, race, economics, and more. It is its own form of diversity.

Part of my job description in Campus Ministry is to serve the LGBT students at Notre Dame. A few weeks ago I set out to meet individually with 11 LGBT students. I wanted to talk with them one by one, to hear their stories (if they wished to share them), and to ask them if they might be willing to come to an afternoon gathering to talk about how Campus Ministry might serve the needs of LGBT students. At each meeting I explained the purpose of the afternoon meeting to which I would invite them.

I am interested in meeting with students at Notre Dame who are LGBT and are people of faith, who are trying to figure out how to make these two things connect and intersect. What is the intersection of spirituality and sexuality? How can Helen be both 100% Lesbian and 100% Catholic? How can Bill be Catholic to the core and yet very open about being bisexual? How can our LGBT students be who they are and practice their faith? I explained that the purpose of the meeting is not to talk about policies or platforms or that sort of thing. Rather I would listen to what these beautiful children of God want of the Church, what they want of Campus Ministry, and I would try to respond.

I think that it's impossible to listen to the painful stories of gay and lesbian people without being converted. That is to say, in truly listening to these stories, we have to think differently. In listening to anyone's story we are changed, we are converted.

I received an e-mail from a student who heard about my meetings with individual students. "I was so pleased to hear from Paul that this was an issue on your mind and one that you are willing to address. I have often felt the LGBT representation and message spread on campus to be a bit disjointed, and I think working in collaboration with Campus Ministry will afford an excellent opportunity for young Catholic men and women to explore how their faith will intersect with their sexuality."

I am interested in this ministry for many reasons. If our LGBT students do not find a home in the Church—or worse, feel disrespected by the Church—they will leave the Church. Sadly, this happens all too often...and then nobody wins. They lose and the Church loses. They leave the Church and live without the Sacraments and the life of the Church. And the Church is weakened by their departure. A part of the face of Christ is absent from the Church. A part of the Body of Christ is missing. No one wins.

The language from the Church about LGBT people has not been good. At times it has been awful, dreadful, and often completely bereft of mercy. The world is getting better at this but I don't think that the world can understand why faith might be so important to an LGBT person, especially to an LGBT person who wants to live in a Church which has often treated them unfairly, shunned them, and not understood them. The Church must make every effort to understand what it means to be LGBT and Catholic.

I was not surprised to find students who genuinely

want to live their faith and want to be Catholic while not having to deny who God created them to be. How to be Catholic and to be LGBT is a big question, but answers can be found if we listen to each other's stories and if we commit to really working at it.

I love the Church. I love the Church with all my heart and soul. I am a son of the Church. I want to die in the arms of the Church. I have hoped for a long time that the Church might take the lead on this issue—on understanding and accepting and explaining what it is to be LGBT and Catholic.

Sadly, the Church is often the caboose of the train when it comes time to change its views. My hope is that it might be the engine on some things where thinking needs to change, like this one. I cannot understand why the Church drags its feet on this issue. For years the Church has said that there are certain people born with a homosexual orientation. Well, then…this is a conflict in search of resolution, and it has implications for all of us sinners in need of mercy.

Jesus invites us, regardless of sexual orientation, to love one another. There are many ways to love and to give ourselves to one another, to sacrifice for one another, to help each other build up the Body of Christ. No one gets a pass from the Lord's invitation to love one another. *That* we love one another is more important than *how* we love one another.

The mercy of God invites us to listen to one another, to hear each other's stories, to share each other's joys and sorrows. We are all children of God. All of us—straight or LGBT or anywhere in between—need the mercy of God and are called to extend that mercy. As Pope Francis has said so often during the Year of Mercy, "No one is excluded from the mercy of God." No one has to be other than who they are to receive this mercy from God. It is available to all of us as we are.

Lord Jesus Christ, Son of the Living God,
have mercy on me, a sinner.

Continuing Thoughts

When Pope Francis closed the Holy Door on November 20, 2016, signifying the end of the Extraordinary Jubilee Year of Mercy, he said: "Mercy cannot become a mere parenthesis in the life of the Church; it constitutes her very existence, through which the profound truths the Gospel are made manifest and tangible. Everything is revealed in mercy; everything is resolved in the merciful love of the Father." And so it is. The mercy of God is the foundation of the Church. I especially love the phrase "everything is resolved in the merciful love of the Father." There are things that cannot be understood, reconciled, or explained in this life. So it helps me to think that they can all be resolved in the merciful love of the Father.

How do we keep the year of mercy alive? Perhaps the primary way is to make the corporal and spiritual works of mercy a way of life.

The corporal works of mercy are:

Feed the hungry
Give drink to the thirsty
Shelter the homeless
Visit the sick
Visit prisoners
Bury the dead
Give alms to the poor

And the spiritual works of mercy are:

Counsel the doubtful
Instruct the ignorant
Admonish the sinner
Comfort the sorrowful
Forgive injuries
Bear wrongs patiently
Pray for the living and the dead

What the corporal and spiritual works of mercy have in common is that, in one way or another, they put us in touch with other people and their life stories and journeys—hence, the ability to practice what Pope Francis calls the culture of encounter. The culture of encounter, as noted previously, simply means this: "You have something good to give to me, and I have something good to give to you." Think about this. What would the world be like, what would we be like, if we all approached one another with this way of thinking? You have something good to give to me, and I have something good to give to you.

What would society be like if we related to one another person to person, with good to receive and good to give, rather than rich to poor, documented to undocumented, educated to non-educated, gay to straight, priest to lay people, Christian to Muslin, but truly person to person, human to human. You have something good to give to me, and I have something good to give to you.

Not only would we recognize that we are all connected, not only would we realize that we are all part of one another, not only would we know our oneness in God, but we also would all recognize our common need for mercy—no matter who we are, no matter what we do, no matter what we have done or not done, no matter if we are the older brother or the younger brother or both brothers in the Parable of the Merciful Father, we would know our common need for mercy. And knowing our common need for mercy would reduce or possibly even eliminate our divisions. For sure we would be able to be more open and understanding and accepting of one another. My Novice Master used to say that, if you were to set everyone's life story to music, you would recognize the melody everywhere.

I will be forever grateful to Pope Francis for calling me and sending me to serve as a Missionary of Mercy. The only claim that I have for this is that I am a sinner whose sins are forgiven. It is from and in this self-understanding that I have tried to serve the Church as a Missionary of Mercy. And it is from this that I have written and shared these reflections.

I hope in reading them and in thinking about them and in praying over them that you might allow this mercy to enter your life more fully and more deeply. Though we might tire of asking God for forgiveness, God never tires of offering us forgiveness. Pope Francis writes, "God is merciful (cf. *Ex* 34:6); his mercy lasts forever (cf. *Ps* 136). From generation to generation, it embraces all those who trust in him and it changes them, by bestowing a share in his very life."

Lord Jesus Christ, Son of the Living God,
have mercy on me, a sinner.

About the Author

Father Joe Corpora, C.S.C., will be grateful to God forever for the gift of a vocation to the priesthood in the Congregation of Holy Cross. Fr. Joe was raised in Easton, Pennsylvania where he attended St. Anthony Grade School (K-8) and Easton Area High School (9-12). He enrolled at the University of Notre Dame in 1972. Following graduation in 1976, he entered the seminary and was ordained to the priesthood in 1984. He served six years at the University of Portland in Portland, Oregon. In 1990, he was transferred to St. John Vianney Parish in Goodyear, Arizona, where he served as Pastor until 2002. Then he was transferred to Holy Redeemer Parish in Portland, Oregon, where he served as Pastor from 2002-2009. In 2009, he was transferred to his alma mater, where he currently works in the Alliance for Catholic Education, in Campus Ministry, and is a priest in residence in Dillon Hall. In December of 2015, Pope Francis appointed him as a Missionary of Mercy. He continues to serve in this role. Father Joe is a sinner whose sins are forgiven—and he loves anything made with tomato sauce!